SOCIONOMICS

How Social Mood Shapes Society

Mikko Ketovuori

Routledge
Taylor & Francis Group

LONDON AND NEW YORK

Designed cover image: Mario Merz, Fibonacci Sequence 1–55, 1994. Turku, Finland

First published 2024
by Routledge
4 Park Square, Milton Park, Abingdon, Oxon OX14 4RN

and by Routledge
605 Third Avenue, New York, NY 10158

Routledge is an imprint of the Taylor & Francis Group, an informa business

British Library Cataloguing-in-Publication Data
A catalogue record for this book is available from the British Library

ISBN: 978-1-032-48069-5 (hbk)
ISBN: 978-1-032-48070-1 (pbk)
ISBN: 978-1-003-38723-7 (ebk)

DOI: 10.4324/9781003387237

Typeset in Sabon
by codeMantra

SOCIONOMICS

Socionomics: How Social Mood Shapes Society explores the main principles and applications of socionomic theory as elaborated by Robert Prechter. Socionomic theory posits that an omnipresent social mood, shifting constantly in a wave form through society, is responsible for the aggregate tenor and character of all social, economic and cultural trends, from fluctuations in the stock market to the popularity of particular genres of music at a given time.

The social mood as an endogenous and collective disposition has its roots in the herding instinct often identified amongst crowds. Individuals typically make rational decisions when acting alone, and in the context of certainty, but in groups and in context of uncertainty, mood-based mimetic behavior can affect all the participants. As social mood often goes unnoticed, people tend to give their collective feelings labels to rationalize them, thus constituting 'public opinion'. Therefore, whilst 'public opinion' as presented in the media is usually seen as rational, it is in fact based on the social mood context that often determines how people think, feel and behave. As the internet and social media have become ubiquitous in our daily lives, these rationalizations are spreading faster and faster than ever before and creating a pseudo-reality which can corrupt the collective perception of what is real and what is not.

This stimulating and thought-provoking book will be of great interest to academics, practitioners and policymakers with an interest in the humanities and social sciences, particularly sociology and economics.

Mikko Ketovuori is a University Lecturer in the Department of Teacher Education at the University of Turku, Finland. His research interests include the theory and application of socionomics and herd theory as well as education theory and policy and the role of the arts in society. He is the author of numerous journal articles and conference papers and, as a keynote speaker and lecturer, he has given lectures across Asia, Europe and North America.

To Heli, Sara & Lauri

CONTENTS

FIGURES

TABLES

INTRODUCTION

The subject of this book, Robert Prechter's theory of socionomics, is not yet widely known among scholars or the general public. The readers who are already familiar with it are likely to have studied either futurology or are interested in technical analysis of finance and probably have also used it in their investment activities. However, the core of the theory is much broader than its practical applications in the financial markets. Socionomics explores the phenomena of history, psychology, biology, sociology, macroeconomics, finance, the arts and entertainment, politics, and war - to list but some of its domains. The cornucopia of its research findings offers surprising conclusions that are often unique and at odds with everyday thinking. Just as the theory differs from conventional views of economics and finance, it also differs from the most known behavioral theories.

According to socionomics, the social trends that define history are regulated not by reason but by social mood, which is expressed through the herding instinct. Even though this herding instinct is an integral part of humanity, social mood is rarely perceived, and if it is sometimes noticed, only a few are willing to admit that it affects them. In general, we tend to think that humans are rational beings in their social endeavors. Historians and contemporary commentators may propose rational bases for the tenor and character of societal trends, but socionomics argues that such accounts are rationalizations, i.e., although commentators purport to explain the phenomena retrospectively, the real causes are based on the prevailing social mood.[1]

Usually if people have heard of Prechter, it is for method of technical financial market analysis called the Elliott Wave Principle. Prechter did not discover the Wave Principle, but he is responsible for popularizing it as a form of market analysis in the 1970s and 1980s. In the 1930s, Ralph Nelson Elliott

DOI: 10.4324/9781003387237-1

(1871–1948) studied and modeled the movements of the Dow Jones Industrial Average over a 75-year history, finding them to follow regularities – later called Elliott waves. While stock market prices may seem random and unpredictable, Elliott said the wave structure makes it possible to predict the ups and downs of stock prices. Elliott discovered that stock market prices fluctuate in a fractal manner, though the term "fractal" had yet to be coined.[2] He presented the theory he developed in two books, *The Wave Principle* (1938) and *Nature's Law – The Secret of the Universe* (1946).

Three decades after Elliott's death, a handful of practitioners continued to publish market commentary using his method. Yet Elliott's original writings may have been lost to history if Prechter had not rediscovered them in the 1970s. While searching for the original manuscripts, Prechter found that Elliott's works were absent from the Library of Congress in Washington, D.C. He finally found them stored on microfilm at the New York City Library.[3] In the hands of Prechter, Elliott's original work and ideas came to a wider consciousness. Today, Elliott wave analysis is among the most popular forms of technical market analysis in the world.

While Prechter worked to popularize and apply Elliott's theory, he also developed his own ideas. His socionomic theory subsumes the Wave Principle and presents a detailed account and theoretical framework for how social mood regulates the tenor and character of social trends. The development of this profound idea has continued across six decades, eventually leading to the creation of a research institute, a printing house and a market analysis firm, as well as a collection of books, papers and articles on the issue. Prechter's main production and research can be divided into following categories:

Books on financial market analysis and forecasting:

- *Elliott Wave Principle: Key to Market Behavior.* (1978) Frost & Prechter. Introduction by Charles J. Collin's
- *R.N. Elliott's Masterworks* (originally titled *The Major Works of R.N. Elliott*, 1980)
- *R.N. Elliott's Market Letters, 1938–1946* (1993)
- *The Complete Elliott Wave Writings of A. Hamilton Bolton and Charles J. Collins* (1994)
- *The Basics of the Elliott Wave Principle* (1995)
- *At the Crest of the Tidal Wave: A Forecast for the Great Bear Market* (1995)
- *The Elliott Wave Writings of A.J. Frost and Richard Russell* (1996)
- *Conquer the Crash: You Can Survive and Prosper in a Deflationary Depression* (2002)
- *Market Analysis for the New Millennium* (2002)
- *View from the Top of the Grand Supercycle* (2003)
- *Beautiful Pictures from the Gallery of Phinance* (2003)
- *How to Forecast Gold and Silver Using the Wave Principle* (2006)

- *The Mania Chronicles: A Real-Time Account of the Great Financial Bubble* (with Peter Kendall, 2009)
- *Last Call* (2022)
- *Forecast for the Bear, 2022–2024 and Beyond* (2022)

Books on socionomics, culture and society[4]:

- *The Wave Principle of Human Social Behavior and the New Science of Socionomics* (1999)
- *Pioneering Studies in Socionomics* (2003)
- *The Socionomic Theory of Finance* (2016)
- *Socionomic Studies of Society and Culture—How Social Mood Shapes Trends from Film to Fashion* (2017)
- *Socionomic Causality in Politics—How Social Mood Influences Everything from Elections to Geopolitics* (2017)

In addition to financial markets and socionomics, Prechter has written 25 research articles on the life and works of Edward de Vere, the 17th Earl of Oxford. Prechter's studies of de Vere culminated in a 24-volume project entitled Oxford's Voices (2021), which took 24 years to research and write. While this specific line of inquiry is unrelated to the development of socionomics, I will demonstrate later that Prechter's understanding of major trends in the arts generally was crucial to his formation of socionomic theory.

Since no thoughts arise in a vacuum, Prechter's theory is also tied to his personal history. Prechter graduated from Yale University in 1971 with a degree in psychology. Starting in high school, though, he had also begun to develop an interest in financial markets. Thus socionomics logically combines his interests in markets and psychology. Prechter was unconvinced by the macroeconomic theories he encountered in his economics classes at the university. From a psychologist's point of view, the economy is about people, not some kind of machine that could be controlled by rules like a system in physics. Prechter's conclusion was clear: the explanations that economists gave for fluctuations in the financial markets and economy were ex-post rationalizations. If the economists were rationalizing, maybe the economy was not controlled by reason.

Prechter also became interested in investment matters in practice. Following a tip from his father, he invested in South African gold stocks. Within 16 months, Prechter's investments in West Rand and Orange Free State yielded a 400% return. Pursuing a career on Wall Street may have been an easy decision after a successful investment start. Before moving to the Street, however, Prechter experimented with a career as a musician playing drums in his own band for four years. Prechter's passion for music, too, would play a role in the birth of socionomics.

While he gigged as a musician, Prechter further explored, developed and applied ideas relating to financial market behavior in real-world markets.

The first time he put Elliott's theory into practice as a trader was in December 1974, when he sold his gold positions within a day of a significant top in the market. He turned bullish on the stock market and began buying shares of six companies the following month. The stock market would rally strongly for six months, while gold would fall by nearly half over the next year and a half. Another trade came a year later, in December 1975, when the stock market began to turn higher again. Prechter bought a large number of call options with astounding results. In just a few months, he had made more than ten times his investment.[5]

1975 was also the year that Prechter said began his Wall Street career, joining the Market Analysis Department at Merrill Lynch under the guidance of the famed investor and analyst Robert J. Farrell. In 1976, he began publishing financial market commentary. His first book, *Elliott Wave Principle—Key to Market Behavior*, co-authored with A.J. Frost, would follow in 1978. The next year, he left Wall Street to found Elliott Wave International, where he has published market analysis in his monthly publication, *The Elliott Wave Theorist*, ever since.

In 1984, Prechter won the U.S. Stock Trading Championship with a then-record 444% return.[6] This achievement was based on approximately 200 short-term trades he made while monitoring hourly market data for four months. With this achievement, his reputation grew. Contrary to the nearly unanimous pessimistic view of economists and professional investors at the time, Prechter also came to predict the stock market's dramatic rise in the 1980s, writing in April 1983 that the bull market:

> should be characterized, at its end, by an almost unbelievable institutional mania for stocks and a public mania for stock index futures, stock options, and options on futures. In my opinion, the long-term sentiment gauges will give off major trend sell signals two or three years before the final top, and the market will just keep on going. In order for the Dow to reach the heights expected by the year 1987 or 1990, *and* in order to set up the U.S. stock market to experience the greatest crash in its history, which, according to the Wave Principle, is due to follow wave V, investor mass psychology should reach manic proportions, with elements of 1929, 1968 and 1973 all operating together and, at the end, to an even greater extreme.[7]

In accordance with this forecast, a stock market mania developed in the ensuing years, and the biggest stock market crash in U.S. history indeed followed in 1987 when the Dow Jones Industrial Average lost 22.6% in a single day. In 1989, the Financial News Network (now CNBC) named Prechter "Guru of the Decade". As Prechter explained in *Conquer the Crash* (2002), after successfully forecasting the historic financial mania, he nevertheless "jumped off the train too early" and became long-term bearish in the wake of the 1987 crash. As Keynes said, "the market can remain irrational longer than you can remain solvent". In the 1970s and 1980s, Prechter developed a well-established reputation as a bull. As the 1990s wore on, he gradually developed the opposite reputation, that of a permanent bear.

In the book *At the Crest of the Tidal Wave* (1995), Prechter's view became clear. It would only be a matter of time before a long-lasting rise in the stock market turned into a huge decline. The devastating bursting of the tech mania followed from 1998–2002. Prechter followed up in 2002 with *Conquer the Crash*, which became a *New York Times* bestseller and predicted the deflationary conditions that would ultimately materialize in the 2008 financial crisis. These financial and economic developments came as a complete surprise to many economists. When Queen Elizabeth II later asked economics experts why they did not predict the global financial crisis, they readily admitted that it was due to a lack of collective imagination and an inability to understand systemic risks as a whole.[8] In socionomic theory, however, the use of imagination and systemic thinking are already necessities.

In addition, understanding socionomic theory requires analogical thinking, in which seemingly separate things are juxtaposed, and their similarity and equivalence are examined. Since all aggregate behavioral trends in society are essentially manifestations of the mood of the crowd, they often resemble each other and fluctuate similarly. The common denominator behind these phenomena is the social mood, and its influence on the world is transmitted through the human herding instinct. Social mood varies over time, dynamically fluctuating in waves of optimism and pessimism. The Socionomics Institute formulated the five tenets of socionomics,[9] as follows:

1 Social mood motivates social actions, not the other way around.
2 Social mood is endogenously regulated, not prompted by outside forces.
3 Social mood is constantly fluctuating according to a hierarchical, robust fractal called the Wave Principle. Robust fractals are patterned but quantitatively variable.
4 Social mood is unconscious and unremembered.
5 Waves of social mood arise when humans interact socially. The process appears to be related to the herding impulse.

These rather abstract principles become much clearer when viewed through concrete examples. Robert Prechter tells of a breakthrough in his own thinking in 1975 when he worked as an analyst on Wall Street:

> I was perusing a wall chart of the stock market and thinking about the tonal changes in Beatles records that occurred in 1965–1966. That led me to thinking about popular music in general, which I knew very well. I suddenly perceived that the musical styles I knew about had ebbed and flowed with the stock market. That's when I first had the feeling that I had perceived something important.[10]

In what other area of life would the herd spirit appear as clearly as in popular culture? The screaming of the audience – Beatlemania – the popularity and adoration of the Beatles, on the one hand, and the subsequent expressions of hatred towards the band, on the other, were clear external signs of shifts in the social mood. Those shifts in mood also appeared in the band's music and the lyrics of their songs. In his groundbreaking study of the Beatles (2010), Prechter[11] highlights features of mass culture that I have summarized below and compared to the five tenets outlined earlier:

1 Becoming a phenomenon ambition, circumstance, and the right timing after the breakthrough, the popularity of the band is regulated by social mood. (Compare: Social mood motivates social actions, not the other way around.)
2 Performing artists cannot bring happiness to their society – they can only reflect and symbolize it. (Compare: Social mood is endogenously regulated, not prompted by outside forces.)
3 The significance of a phenomenon can be measured in terms of its prevalence, intensity and duration. (Compare: Social mood is constantly fluctuating according to a hierarchical, robust fractal called the Wave Principle. Robust fractals are patterned but quantitatively variable.)
4 The herding instinct affects even people who seek to resist it. (Social mood is unconscious and unremembered.)
5 Extremes in social mood produce extreme social phenomena. One such manifestation is society's euphoric adulation of pop music icons at positive extremes in the social mood trend.

Prechter began to tie together his observations about the link between social mood, financial market trends and trends in popular music, fashion, and other forms of pop culture in the 1985 essay, "Popular Culture and the Stock Market." Prechter would return to the subject of mood, music and markets later in his career, including in chapters in his 1999 book, *The Wave Principle of Human Social Behavior and the New Science of Socionomics*, and the aforementioned 2010 socionomic study of the Beatles. Beatlemania, as John Lennon described it in 1965, resembled a tribal rite. This mass hysteria was out of anyone's control and at times it also had quite scary features. According to George Harrison, crowds wanted to "go mad" and used the band as an excuse to do it. In fact, often the only ones who were able to maintain even some sense at their concerts were the musicians themselves.

Because popular music reflects its time, its shades tell us about the atmosphere of different periods. The bright and optimistic tone of the music of the 1960s and 1980s reflects the booms of the time. The early 1960s and the 1980s were periods of economic booms with soaring stock markets. The 1970s was a period of economic malaise and financial market stagnation.

However, these indicators – music, financial markets and the economy – do not cause or explain each other. Under socionomic theory, psychologically endogenous trends in social mood regulate all three, along with numerous other aspects of society.

Of course, socionomists have examined much more than just applications to financial markets and music. In fact, socionomics' applications are so vast that it is a rather challenging field to encapsulate in a short volume. To do that, some highly intriguing themes will have to be left out. But that is only because some even more intriguing themes will be left in: On the subject of politics, this book presents geopolitical applications, including a socionomic account of the rise of authoritarianism. On the cultural side, the book talks about James Bond films, popular slang and children's names. It also examines the history of social attitudes regarding drug policy and university education. Toward the end of the book, there are discussions about the media and the social mood, as well as social mood's influence on the history of infectious diseases and the environmental movement. Many popular topics, such as the popularity of sports and car brands, or even broader movie topics, unfortunately remain at the level of short mentions.

Whether we consider the outcome of a presidential election or the emergence of a new popular cinematic genre, socionomic theory says that there's always order behind what may appear to be social chaos. In its kaleidoscopes, socionomics offers numerous perspectives that are rarely seen elsewhere or would even be thought to consider together. The theory is also rare in the sense that it is able to forecast its own popularity relative to other financial and macroeconomic theories.[12] That is because popular financial theories, like musical styles, reflect the social mood of their time.

The Socionomics Institute, founded by Prechter in Gainesville, Georgia, works closely with Elliott Wave International. The Socionomics Institute analyzes how social mood regulates cultural trends. Elliott Wave International analyzes how social mood regulates financial markets. It prepares and sells market analyses of the prices of stocks, currencies, bonds, commodities and various other assets in Europe, Asia and the United States. However, Prechter's public appearances and interviews on television channels such as Bloomberg and CNBC focus primarily on financial and macroeconomic issues, leaving less attention to the cultural side of socionomic theory.

Simultaneously, socionomic theory is just beginning to become known in the university world, although Prechter has lectured on the subject at several well-known universities, including Cambridge, Oxford, MIT (Massachusetts Institute of Technology) and the London School of Economics. Prechter's 2012 socionomic study of presidential elections was the third-most downloaded paper of the year on the Social Science Research Network. The books *Socionomic Causality in Politics* and *Socionomic Studies of Society and Culture* were #1 Amazon bestsellers in behavioral psychology and social theory, respectively. A number of socionomical papers have been published in peer-reviewed journals. A couple of universities even teach socionomic theory as a subject or course. Yet socionomics is a theory that is likely to gain greater popularity when social mood becomes more negative. That's when the theory predicts that people – scholars and the public alike – will become more open to challenging the status quo and embracing theories that account for dynamic social change.

When I first personally became acquainted with Prechter's thinking, the contradiction between the ideas presented in his book *Conquer the Crash* and the prevailing consensus in my home country Finland, could hardly have been bigger. In the summer of 2006, there was a positive mood and faith in the future. The external signs of the prevailing mood were the Eurovision victory by Mr. Lordi, successes in the Olympics and ice hockey World Championships and the strong rise in Nokia's stock price.[13] Also, President Tarja Halonen was elected to her second term – according to socionomics, incumbents are more likely to be re-elected if social mood is positive.[14]

After reading Prechter's book, I realized that the international financial crisis was closer than any mainstream financial commentator would guess. When the Bear Stearns investment bank in the United States collapsed in 2008, I watched with interest to see what would happen next. The key events of that time are documented in the interesting films *Too Big to Fail*[15] and *The Big Short*.[16]

Since Prechter's thoughts fascinated me, I made direct contact with the Socionomics Institute in Georgia. In 2018, Matt Lampert, who was then the Institute's director of research, and I wrote a research article that was published in the journal *Popular Music* by Cambridge University Press.[17] Our article, "From 'Hard Rock Hallelujah' to 'Ukonhauta' in Nokialand: a socionomic perspective on the mood shift in Finland's popular music from 2006 to 2009", dealt with the changing social mood in Finland and how one can measure changes in mood from pop music. Our article is still relevant: many themes that emerged during the financial crisis are not sustainably resolved, and, more broadly, social mood's external societal and cultural signs are abundant, as anyone can see them.

The working title of this book was for a long time "why is the world (always) berserk and messed up?" – even in the best of times, there are parts of the world where social fear, deep pessimism and the rise of authoritarianism are visible. Understanding the mood and of nations is vital to understand why that is the case. While we may hope for more serene times, in today's volatile world, socionomics is much easier to comprehend today than before, as it seems that the theory has become an increasingly relevant description of how the world currently looks. Even though this book was first written in Finnish and intended for a Finnish audience, the references, however, were mostly in English. Updating the book was an obvious choice for reaching larger audiences and the topic was so interesting that the work had to be tackled. Since the publication of the first edition of the Finnish version, new and significant research has been also published on Prechter's theory.

Thank you also to The Association of Finnish Nonfiction Writers that provided financial support; to Mr. Chris Parry and Helen Pritt from Routledge, Assunta Petrone from codeMantra, Jason Lureman from EWI and Lippo Luukkonen as well as my daughter Sara, who studied data analytics and graduated from Georgia Tech during the writing process of this book.

Ten theses for understanding socionomic theory

1 Social mood is a shared state of mind that fluctuates in time dynamically between optimism and pessimism. In its nature, social mood is endogenous, collective, preconscious and rational. Nothing "impacts" social mood, rather its trends and changes unfold naturally.
2 Arational and non-rational thinking differs qualitatively from rational and irrational thinking. People who act non-rationally base their actions on an intuitive impulse to follow the herd.
3 Mood-motivated decisions are non-rational, but people generate rationalizations to justify them after the fact.
4 Social mood is always present in society.
5 Social mood influences changes in a society's political discourse, attitudes and values.
6 Social mood is unremembered and, absent a socionomic perspective, often left unnoticed. That is why certain societal phenomena are repeated time after time: "We learn from history that we do not learn from history".
7 Social mood is reflected in the events, news and atmosphere of the society. Concretely, it affects how we spend our time, the things we believe in, as well as the things that draw our attention.
8 When social mood reaches extremes, correspondingly extreme social events follow. Similarly, as the social mood trend becomes less extreme, so do the tenor and character of corresponding events and trends.
9 Social mood influences the kinds of technologies that society creates and embraces, along with society's uses of existing technology.
10 Social mood cannot be altered, but an individual can learn to act in a manner that deviates from prevailing trends.

Notes

1 In other words, human endeavors are based on mimetic feelings.
2 This was done by Benoit Mandelbrot in 1975.
3 Kendall (1996/2018, 8).

4 The series Socionomics—The Science of History and Social Prediction comprises these five volumes.
5 Kendall (1996/2018, 8–9).
6 Grillo (2009).
7 Prechter, R. (1983, April) A rising tide: the case for wave V in the Dow Jones industrial average. *The Elliott Wave Theorist*, Special Report, p. 6.
8 Chorafas (2013).
9 Prechter 2017, viii.
10 Prechter (2016, 781).
11 Prechter (2010/2017, 3–56).
12 More on this in the chapter on economics.
13 See: https://socionomics.net/2014/01/qa-mikko-ketovuori-on-nokia-pop-music-and-socionomics/
14 Prechter et al. (2012).
15 Directed by Curtis Hanson, 2011. HBO.
16 Directed by Adam McKay, 2015. Paramount Pictures.
17 Republished 2019 in Mood interdisciplinary perspectives, new theories ed. Birgit Breidenbach and Thomas Docherty by Routledge.

References

Chorafas, D.N. (2013). Queen Elizabeth II and the Economists. In: *The Changing Role of Central Banks*. Palgrave Macmillan, New York. https://doi.org/10.1057/9781137332288_2

Grillo, J. (2009). *Gainesville guru*. Georgia Trend. October 1. https://www.georgiatrend.com/2009/10/01/gainesville-guru/.

Kendall, P. (1996/2018) *Prechter's perspective*. Gainesville, GA: New Classics Library.

Prechter, R. (2010) "Social Mood Regulates the Popularity of Stars—Cases in Point: The Beatles." *The Elliott Wave Theorist*, July–August 2010. Reprinted as chapter 1 in: Prechter, R.R. (2017). *Socionomic Studies of Society and Culture: How Social Mood Shapes Trends from Film to Fashion*. Gainesville, GA: Socionomics Institute Press.

Prechter, R.R. (2016) *The socionomic theory of finance*. Gainesville, GA: Socionomics Institute Press.

Prechter, Jr., R.R., Goel, D., Parker, W., and Lampert, M. (2012). Social mood, stock market performance, and U.S. presidential elections. *SAGE Open*. https://doi.org/10.1177/2158244012459194.

1

SOCIAL MOOD AND HERDING

Whoever be the individuals that compose it, however like or unlike be their mode of life, their occupations, their character, or their intelligence, the fact that they have been transformed into a crowd puts them in possession of a sort of collective mind which makes them feel, think, and act in a manner quite different from that in which each individual of them would feel, think, and act were he in a state of isolation.

Le Bon (1895, 15)

According to Robert Prechter's socionomic theory, social mood is an unconscious shared mental disposition that regulates the nature of aggregate trends in society.[1] Social mood is endogenous, ever present and fluctuates in patterned waves. As these waves of social mood unfold, they shape people's behaviors, attitudes and values, ultimately regulating trends in society as a whole. Even though social mood is expressed through herding, most of the time people are not aware of it. Because the power of social mood is stronger than individual mood and emotions, it reaches out and affects us all – despite our mode of life, occupation, character or intelligence as famously stated by Le Bon.

Figure 1.1, reprinted from Lampert (2023), depicts six phases of social mood as it fluctuates from a negative extreme to a positive extreme and back again.[2] These phases are as follows: mood less negative, mood waxing positive, positive mood extreme, mood less positive, mood waxing negative and negative mood extreme. Each of these phases has its own character and features. In the *mood less negative* phase, social mood is still quite negative overall though it is becoming less negative than it was at the prior negative

DOI: 10.4324/9781003387237-2

Social Mood Phases

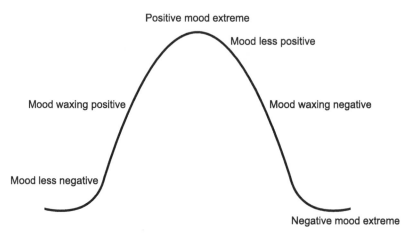

FIGURE 1.1 Social mood phases (Lampert 2023, 3, which itself is a revised version of a Figure originally published in Hayden, A. (2019). From your editor. *The Socionomist*, June 2019, p. 1.)

mood extreme. As this transitional phase continues, one should expect a particularly diverse collection of social mood expressions to come to the fore as the influence of the prior negative mood trend battles with the emerging positive mood trend for dominance. As *mood waxes positive*, negative mood expressions continue to recede in frequency and intensity while positive mood expressions continue to increase in frequency and intensity. As positive mood comes to dominate, the social milieu is associated with happiness, acceptance, inclusion, support and hope. At the *positive mood extreme*, the atmosphere is associated with peaks in confidence, elation and optimism.

From a positive mood extreme, a trend toward negative mood begins. In the *mood less positive* phase, social mood is still quite positive overall though it is becoming less positive than it was at the prior positive mood extreme. As this transitional phase continues, one should expect a particularly diverse collection of social mood expressions to come to the fore as the influence of the prior positive mood trend battles with the emerging negative mood trend for dominance. As *mood waxes negative*, positive mood expressions continue to recede in frequency and intensity while negative mood expressions continue to increase in frequency and intensity. As negative mood comes to dominate, the social milieu is associated with sadness, rejection, exclusion, opposition and despair. At the *negative mood extreme*, the atmosphere is associated with peaks in fear, depression and pessimism. However, from this point, a new trend toward positive mood begins, and the process repeats.

Since social mood influences society's hopes and fears, studying it enables us to analyze the current state of society and its possible futures. Changes in social mood determine changes in the aggregate tenor and character of social expressions. Traits associated with these social expressions can be broadly described using polarities, such as the ones presented in Table 1.1 which is taken from the 2018 printing of Prechter (1999a).

TABLE 1.1 Aspects of social polarity

Positive Mood	*Negative Mood*
Acceptance	Rejection
Accommodation	Obstruction
Adventurousness	Protectionism
Agreeableness	Antagonism
Alignment	Opposition
Allowance	Restriction
Benevolence	Malevolence
Centrism	Extremism
Certainty	Uncertainty
Clarity	Fuzziness
Concord	Discord
Confidence	Fear
Constructiveness	Destructiveness
Convergence	Polarization
Daring	Defensiveness
Desiring power over nature	Desiring power over people
Elation	Depression
Emancipation	Subjugation
Embrace of effort	Avoidance of effort
Feelings of safety	Feelings of vulnerability
Forbearance	Anger
Friendliness	Hostility
Friskiness	Somberness
Frivolity	Seriousness
Happiness	Unhappiness
Homogeneity	Heterogeneity
Hopefulness	Despair
Inclusion	Exclusion
Interest in love	Interest in sex
Optimism	Pessimism

(*Continued*)

TABLE 1.1 (Continued)

Positive Mood	Negative Mood
Practical thinking	Magical thinking
Responsibility	Blame
Romanticism	Cynicism
Search for joy	Search for pleasure
Self-providence	Self-deprivation
Serenity	Anxiety
Sharpness of focus	Dullness of focus
Supportiveness	Opposition
Sympathy	Meanness
Tendency to excuse	Tendency to accuse
Tendency to praise	Tendency to criticize
Togetherness	Separatism
Trust	Suspicion

As Figure 1.1 illustrates, social mood fluctuates along a spectrum instead of oscillating from a singular positive mood state to a singular negative mood state. As such, social mood expressions are never universally positive or universally negative; there is always a mix (Prechter 2016, 149). The relevant empirical question, then, is to determine the frequency and intensity of positive mood expressions relative to the frequency and intensity of negative mood expressions. As social mood grows more positive, socionomics predicts that social expressions associated with the traits on the left side of Table 1.1 will grow more frequent and intense relative to expressions associated with the traits on the right side. As social mood grows more negative, socionomics predicts that social expressions associated with the traits on the right side of the table will grow more frequent and intense relative to expressions associated with the traits on the left side. Crucially, socionomics proposes that there is no feedback loop from social expressions back to the social mood.[3] The arrow of causality points in one direction from social mood to the aggregate tenor and character of social expressions.

Because the social mood is decisive in terms of the aggregate traits of the decisions that consumers, financiers and companies make, it has a direct effect on the financial markets and the macroeconomy too. When a positive mood prevails, speculators send stock prices higher, businesses expand and the economy grows, whereas when a negative mood prevails, speculators send stock prices lower, businesses contract and the economy shrinks. According to socionomics, the stock market reflects society's social mood – not the fundamental value of companies, as traditional finance teaches. As such, socionomists often use stock market indexes as benchmark "sociometers" or social mood indicators.

As the basis of the herding instinct and social mood is biological, the human's natural tendency to form and act in social groups likely emanates from the limbic system of the human brain. The limbic brain regulates both a person's autonomic functions and emotions, while the neocortex is in charge of rational decision-making. However, the latter system is weaker than the former. According to Daniel Kahneman's *Thinking, Fast and Slow* the impulsive, instinctive and non-rational mind is faster than the deliberative, contemplative and rational mind. Socionomics proposes that the impulsive and non-rational mind swiftly and spontaneously expresses social mood, and the deliberative, rational mind fabricates a rationalization for what the non-rational mind demands.

On an individual level, rationalization is seen as a reactive tendency to explain things and express opinions about affairs—whether in everyday news, daily encounters with different people or in social media—in a manner that is blind to the influence of social mood. People constantly use rationalization as an excuse even for their own feelings. By rationalizing, people think that they are reasonable. Rational or not, people rationalize all the time, and in many cases, even though it might sound like a reasonable choice, the conclusion and its consequences can be completely non-rational, as the following example shows:

> If you believe that a man threatens your life, if you want to live, and if you think he can only be stopped with a bullet, then it is rational to shoot him. Rationalization turns this process on its head: First, you shoot a man, and from this you conclude that he threatened your life.[4]

In short, even though rationalization can be described as a defense mechanism, it is also much more than that. Since all social sciences, from psychology, to sociology to economics and political science, are built on the basic assumption that social events regulate the content and nature of the social mood, the assumption of causality and rationality is so deeply ingrained that it is hardly ever even acknowledged as an assumption. Rationalization is thus a structured way of thinking that guides our reasoning automatically. Socionomics challenges this by turning the model of explanation on its head by reversing the orthodox ways of thinking and inverting exogenous explanations into endogenous ones, as seen in the following table:

TABLE 1.2 Mechanical and socionomical causality (Prechter 2004/2018)

Mechanical causality (exogeneous cause)	Socionomic causality (endogenous cause)
Social events determine the tenor and character of social mood	Social mood determines the tenor and character of social events.
• Recession causes businesspeople to be cautious.	• Cautious businesspeople cause recession.
• Talented leaders make the population happy.	• A happy population makes leaders appear talented.

(Continued)

TABLE 1.2 (Continued)

Mechanical causality (exogeneous cause)	Socionomic causality (endogenous cause)
• A rising stock market makes people increasingly optimistic.	• Increasingly optimistic people make the stock market rise.
• Scandals make people outraged.	• Outraged people seek out scandals
• The availability of derivates fosters a desire to speculate.	• A desire to speculate fosters the availability of derivates.
• War makes people fearful and angry.	• A fearful and angry people make war.
• Epidemics cause society to be fearful and depressed.	• A depressed and fearful society is susceptible to epidemics.
• Happy music makes people smile.	• People who want to smile choose happy music.
• Nuclear bomb testing makes people nervous.	• Nervous people test nuclear bombs.
• The success of financial television spurred excitement among investors.	• Excited investors spurred the success of financial television.
• An expanding economy puts people in a good mood.	• People in a good mood generate an expanding economy.
• Falling markets make investors fearful.	• Fearful investors make markets fall.
• Good news makes stock rise, and bad news make them fall.	• No, it doesn't. They just coincide sometimes.

Even though some of the examples might resemble each other and while some of them do not necessarily seem to be mutually exclusive, the question is as follows: Which of the following statements is more likely true: *happy music makes people smile* or *people, who want to smile choose happy music*? According to Prechter, since people are moved by the social mood, those who want to smile end up listening to happy music. Happy music, of course, might make sad people smile. But what audiences want to listen to depends on the prevailing social mood.[5] When reflected in the external world, the social mood takes concrete shape in various other things and objects, such as the height of skyscrapers or the trendy lengths of skirts. Similarly, the collective events that shape the destinies of nations can be measured and interpreted as indicators of current social trends. Scared and angry people look for scandals, they test nuclear bombs and eventually start wars too.

As Prechter (2016, 120) explains:

Social activity is nevertheless rich in the production of specific responsive and counter-responsive actions, producing the complex dynamic in which events cause events, to which feedback does apply. Specific social events produce chains of other specific social events, stemming from the exercise of both rational and non-rational choices. For example, if negative social mood were to lead one government to attack another's territory, the target

TABLE 1.3 The taxonomy of moods by Casti (2010, 25)

+ Mood rising	+ Mood peak	— Mood declining	— Mood bottom
Hope	Hubris	Fear	Despair

government would respond, other governments would choose sides, soldiers would be drafted, families would become fatherless, and so on … Social mood does not regulate these changes directly, but it eventually results
in them. … None of these subsequent events, however, feeds back to affect
the endogenously and autonomously regulated fluctuations in social mood.[6]

As both people and nations are affected by the mood-instigated chains of
events, the prime mover *causa prima* beneath history is the endogenously
regulated fluctuation of social mood. The tenor and character of history is
thus socionomically determined, even though the events themselves are cha-
otically determined.[7]

In his interpretation of Prechter's socionomic theory, John Casti conceptu-
alizes social mood as a sum of beliefs a population holds about their future.
The sum of beliefs affects the general direction of a society and its culture. He
presents a taxonomy of four phases of social mood, which he connects with
four corresponding basic emotions.[8] These primary emotions are hope, hubris, fear, and despair, of which hope and fear are the most common emotions.

Casti observes that critical points, where the mood is either at a positive
or negative extreme, form an infinitesimal set of all moments. Therefore,
predicting that the current trend will continue tomorrow (as positive or negative) is usually a correct prediction. The challenge, however, is to predict the
critical points, i.e., the turning points of trends. That knowledge is, when
accurate, worth paying for.[9]

An atmosphere of hope takes hold when social mood is positive. Society
is optimistic, open and tolerant – people try their best and take also risks. As
a consequence of this, success follows. Since optimism cannot last forever,
at some point the trend changes. This is seen in many levels of the society.
People become alienated from the values and principles on which the original
success was based and built upon. The turning point of the trend is seen when
the social mood reaches its positive extreme and hubris supersedes hope. A
sign of this is the loss of the core mission of institutions and companies. Although the external forms of the culture are still visible, the meanings associated with it have already faded. After the positive mood extreme, a turning
point in the mood is reached, and a trend toward negative social mood starts.

As the social mood turns toward the negative, society's faith in itself begins to weaken. Suspicion and fear, polarization, pessimism and discord are
increasing. Centrist beliefs are opposed, and new, more extreme ones are

fiercely sought. At a large-degree negative extreme, the negative social mood eventually leads to economic recession or depression, systemic collapse, and war. After the trend reaches the negative extreme – despair – a new wave of positive mood begins and enables a way out of the situation. Every crisis carries thus the seed of a new opportunity within. This new wave of positive social mood brings about hope.

Although these social mood waves described above are reflected in our personal experience of the world, social mood, individual mood and human emotions are different things.

Mood and emotions

According to Robert Prechter, mood affects emotions, but emotions do not affect mood. Furthermore, there is no feedback loop from social events to the social mood. While emotions are exogenously cued, consciously experienced feelings, regulated by a combination of mood, circumstances, and events, mood, in its turn, is non-referential, unconscious, affective, evaluative and future-oriented disposition in its nature. Mood as a primary instigator of action influences mental processes (thoughts), emotions, perceptions, wishes, desires, attitudes, beliefs, impulses, aspirations and decisions.[10] On its broadest scale, social mood can be understood as a predispositional state, as it is a tendency and potentiality of a group of people for certain types of actions. Social mood motivates social action.[11]

Traditional cognitive psychology's perspective on the matter is much narrower. According to its research tradition, individuals' emotions can be isolated into concepts and words such as anxious, sad, happy, etc. From the view of biology and neuroscience, emotions can be, nowadays, imaged also from the human body and the brain. Brain imaging confirms what William James already in 1890 brought out in his seminal work *The Principles of Psychology* – the mutual relationship between body and cognition cannot be separated from each other. According to James, feelings always precede consciousness, as bodily reactions convey them to a person's mind. Socionomics emphasizes the influence of the mood of the society, which is far greater than the mood of the individual.

Because the words related to emotions are used inconsistently both in the psychological research literature and in everyday speech,[12] the meanings of words such as feeling, affect and emotion and mood vary depending on the context. At the same time, scholars from different disciplines in the humanities and the social and behavioral sciences quite rarely agree on these issues. As a consequence of this, the theoretical and empirical literature on emotions is extremely complex and reflects more controversy than consensus.[13] However, the following labels are often used to delineate emotions: (1) the duration of the phenomenon; (2) whether it is subjective, objective or both; (3) the relative involvement of cognition and (4) the phenomenological level.[14]

Based on this division, it is easy to state that (1) moods and emotions last longer than affects and feelings; (2&3) moods are subjective but unconscious, while feelings and emotions are subjective but more conscious[15] and (4) that while feelings and emotions are at the surface of human experience, the moods lie at a deep level in the collective consciousness. Since social mood accounts for a significant part of people's choices, the combination and influence of social mood and people's emotions are undoubtedly much greater than is generally assumed. The following figure of the layers of human experience, an original contribution of this volume, can be derived from these conclusions.

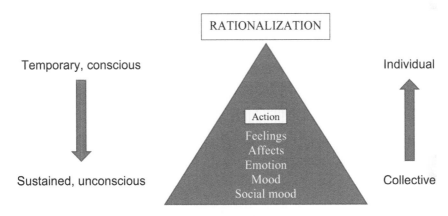

FIGURE 1.2 The layers of human experience.

Although the layers of human experience are drawn in this picture as a hierarchy, setting clear boundaries between different types of emotions and measuring them are obviously a hard task, as the layers are intertwined. The extent to which emotion and reason play a role in decision-making – let alone in human experience – is also a difficult question to answer.[16] However, since social mood is the most sustained of the layers of human experience, it frames all people's experiential being in the world. Social mood is an unconscious disposition, and an individual's moods are often unnoticed non-intentional states that both motivate and guide the human perception. The role of emotion (in Latin *emovere*) is to act as a mediator, bringing up unconscious neural responses, and raising affects that produce fluctuating feelings. Social action and individual decisions are largely based on humans as non-rational beings, even though we like to see ourselves as principally rational beings.[17] That belief itself is rationalization *par excellence*! However, socionomics recognizes a role for rational thought in the human experience. In contexts of knowledge and certainty, people use reason to make decisions.[18]

Yet much of the human experience is marked by contexts of uncertainty or arbitrariness, and thus social mood heavily regulates such aspects of social life. One of the key areas of life is especially interesting in this regard.

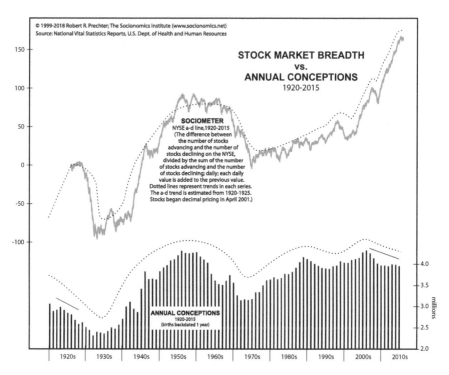

© 1999-2018 Robert R. Prechter; The Socionomics Institute (www.socionomics.net)
Source: National Vital Statistics Reports, U.S. Dept. of Health and Human Resources

STOCK MARKET BREADTH
vs.
ANNUAL CONCEPTIONS
1920-2015

SOCIOMETER
NYSE a-d line, 1920-2015
(The difference between
the number of stocks
advancing and the number of
stocks declining on the NYSE,
divided by the sum of the number
of stocks advancing and the number
of stocks declining; daily; each daily
value is added to the previous value.
Dotted lines represent trends in each series.
The a-d trend is estimated from 1920-1925.
Stocks began decimal pricing in April 2001.)

ANNUAL CONCEPTIONS
1920-2015
(births backdated 1 year)

FIGURE 1.3 Stock market prices vs. births (Thompson, C. (2016). Stocks & sex: revisited. *The Socionomist*, June 2018, p. 3, which itself is an up-dated version of a Figure originally published in Prechter, R. (1999). A socionomic view of demographic trends, or stocks & sex. *The Elliott Wave Theorist*, September 1999, pp. 1–6).

That is the relationship between social mood and births. Prechter (1999b) discovered that usually supposedly causal desires, such as looking for the mate and its results such as marriages, pregnancies and births,[19] seem to follow fluctuation of optimism and pessimism as reflected in benchmark sociometers such as stock market indexes. In Figure 1.3, researchers from the Socionomics Institute updated a chart that appeared in Prechter's original 1999 study. It plots U.S. annual births and the New York Stock Exchange's advance-decline line, a broad measure of stock market performance. When social mood trends toward the positive, aggregate feelings of friskiness, daring and confidence wax, and people send stock prices higher and engage in more sexual activity. The results of the latter show up in demographics approximately nine months later. Correspondingly, when social mood trends toward the negative, these feelings wane, and people engage in the opposite behaviors, resulting in declining stock prices and, eventually, declining births:[20]

Interestingly, in recent years there has been a divergence between the trend of stock prices and births, while the previous indicator has continued its rising and the latter has been in decline. Thompson (2018) noted that the only other time there was a similarly persistent divergence between the advance-decline line and births was in the 1920s before the Great Depression, a striking omen indeed.

Robert Prechter's socionomic research on stocks and births preceded more recent findings on the issue. His conclusion is consistent with recent research, which shows that declining conception might be an early warning for recessions.[21] According to Comolli and Vignoli (2021), spreading uncertainty and shrinking birth rates go hand in hand, while the Bank of England researchers' study (Goodhart and Pradhan 2020) shows that the changes in the age structure and number of the population may have a greater impact on the societies than previously has been thought. According to Lillrank (2021), especially in Japan and Northern Europe, there is likely to be a period when economic development and progress will slow down as the population ages. The challenge is how to decline elegantly and to shrink without causing chaos in the systems and function of society.

As the aforementioned researchers are looking for causal explanations for the declining population, the socionomic question however is: Which comes first, social mood or the detached reasons that are used to explain the spreading uncertainty in populations? As long as explanations are considered through exogenous reasoning, the true cause of the findings remains obscured. The naturally unfolding reason for the decline in birth rates may sound light, trivial or too obvious. People don't have children because they fundamentally are pessimistic and thus, do not want to have them. This reluctance is directly dependent on the prevailing social mood, which is reflected as a lack of faith in the future.

Although reproduction and emotion, like so many other human endeavors in society, are certainly related to social mood, the study of human emotions has been for a long time almost ignored in the humanities, as well as in other social sciences, with the possible exception of psychology. It seems that emotions, affects and feelings have been considered either a private matter or uninteresting and irrelevant for the research of culture and society.

During the last decade, however, the situation has gradually changed. Emotions are now studied by media researchers,[22] educators[23] and administrative researchers,[24] while at the same time in humanistic research the voices in favor of so-called *affective turn* have increased.[25] This new paradigm abandons cognitive Cartesian approach of mind and body dualism. Socionomics, however, opens completely new and even broader perspectives for the discussion by emphasizing the primacy of the social mood over the individual.

A complementary view: arationality, intuition and rationality

If social mood is unconscious, endogenous and so often unnoticed, the question is, how one can examine mood, and what is its ontology? While moods are typically categorized as emotional phenomena they do not still have, unlike emotions, a clear structure of directness toward an object. Moods are not intentional states even though they frame the atmosphere of events, places and histories. They are modalities that intertwine subjective experiences to the world. Moods act as schemas that either limit opportunities or allow the world to emerge in the light of possibilities.[26] For Prechter's socionomic hypothesis, the social mood fluctuates in waves, producing trends in pessimism and optimism.

It is worth emphasizing that in addition to rationality, there are areas of mentation that operate outside of it, such thought is no less valuable or important than rational reasoning – on the contrary, sometimes they can be even more important than mere reasoning. According to Stanford professor Elliott Eisner, the 20th century's educational psychology has separated thinking and feeling from each other, as cognitive activity is seen merely dealing with words and numbers, while emotions, human experience and other social factors are neglected. Since words are considered to be more abstract than images and icons less flexible than propositions, the result of this false conclusion, the arts have been associated with vague feelings and something that might offer satisfaction, but definitely not understanding.[27] As a consequence of this, in school curriculum, rationality is emphasized at the expense of emotion and different activities such as weaving a basket, singing or drawing that are rejected as mindless forms of education compared to algebra, natural sciences and languages. Developing non-rational skills such as sensitive perception, insight and imagination and combining these skills to propositional knowledge, i.e., combining senses to rationality, would be a more balanced approach to educating a human being.

To properly understand the ontology of the mood, the field of arts provides excellent analogies. The emotions and herding instinct, as well as the arts are all derivatives of social mood operating in the context of arational mentation. The socionomic literature employs the term "non-rational" to describe mentation that takes place outside the domain of reason. Researchers in adjacent fields sometimes instead use the term "arational". I use both terms interchangeably. As socionomics sets the mood before rational explanation, also in the arts the mood comes first, then an expression. Whether the cultural expression is a painting, a sculpture or music these objects embody a mood. Only after the shapes become visible, they can be interpreted as reflections of the mood of the era. As art connoisseurs can identify and date an unknown work, naming the painter according to the era, style and the mood of the work, they make use of the processes intuition, arationality and rationality. The judgments are a combination of abduction, comparing previous impressions and evidently, rational decision-making. This balance produces an insightful result.

Could such an ability be useful outside of the field of arts? Sometimes, it can be useful for survival: You are on safari in Africa, and you are staying in a tent. At night you wake up to the rustle of sand and notice something vague. You light the lantern. Its light reveals an unknown reptile to you. An objective, scientific and neutral approach would now require looking at the creature, taking photos of it and making notes for later species identification. Is that species a snake? However, following your arational instinct, you quickly leave the tent.

Socionomics proposes that people think with information in contexts of knowledge and certainty, such as solving a math problem or choosing between purchasing zucchini or broccoli at the supermarket. However, in the context of uncertainty or arbitrariness, social mood plays a greater role in decision-making. The analytical philosophy of the 20th century, "Whereof one cannot speak, thereof one must be silent", i.e., only what can be proved to be either true or false is considered to be knowledge. However, in terms of survival, the arts, or even more importantly, the quality of life itself, such a mere existence based on knowledge remains inexorably narrow. According to socionomic theory, preconscious social mood affects people and groups of people, who constantly interpret the world based on their feelings. This includes a radical claim: in contexts of uncertainty or arbitrariness, people don't think with information; their thoughts and actions are based primarily on their feelings. Important decisions, such as the choice to have children, to pursue a career or expand a business, or how much to pay for a piece of real estate, are regulated at the aggregate level by feeling and intuition, not knowledge. For an individual, this all would require life skills – being a rational independent personality consists of the same characters the art connoisseur has – a strong sense of balance between the three: arationality, intuition and reason. Whether we like it or not, in many contexts the arational mind is more powerful than the rational mind.

Neglecting arationality and only studying the rational mind lead to a woefully incomplete understanding of human behavior, just as much as studying only the arational and neglecting the rational surely would. The influence of social mood is evident in many phenomena in society, as this book will review. Socionomics, although a relatively young field, is opening a completely new paradigm in the social sciences.

Other studies on crowd behavior

The theories of mood can be divided into two categories: whether the theory proposes that mood spreads by contagion vs. if the theory proposes that mood arises. Socionomics is in the latter category, as it proposes that social mood arises naturally when humans interact socially. However, socionomics proposes that the *foci* of social mood, *i.e.*, specific social mood expressions, rationales and cultural referents, can spread by contagion, for example, which investment to own, which pop star to idolize and which enemy to attack.[28] The difference between these two models is that as the contagion metaphor suggests a one-way infection from the sick to the well, or from the better informed to the uninformed, the interaction model suggests that social attitudes and behavior arise from a process of mutual mimicking, where mimickers can produce a behavioral compromise that none of the participants fully expressed at the start. In this matter socionomics stance is clear: in most cases, the contagion model is inadequate and misleading when applied studies of how attitudes arise in society. According to the theory, social mood is a motivator of action, but the forms of action are multiple and variable. The social mood arises (interaction), but rationales spread (contagion). The chain of causality according to Prechter is the following[29]:

- Social mood arises.
- People are induced to express it.
- They identify referents and invent rationales that accommodate mood-induced feelings and justify mood-induced actions.
- And finally, those referents and rationales spread by contagion.

Currently, it is not known how social mood arises from human interaction. Although mimicry is a ubiquitous phenomenon, it often occurs outside of conscious awareness and purpose and is based on communication between the parties, which may include, for example, sight, sound, smells or facial expressions, tone of voice or pheromones.[30]

Researchers outside of socionomics have studied group behavior in many different ways. These studies have been carried out, for example, about depression, happiness, obesity, violence, crime and suicides.[31] The everyday observation of the so-called suicide waves, where the tragedy of one person seems to lead to other similar acts, is confirmed by scientific research.[32] Such studies, though they come from adjacent fields, supplement and shed light on the socionomic hypothesis about the contribution of mood to group behavior of people.

Experimental research,[33] based on emotional contagion theories, has been able to show that positivity is reflected as improved cooperation, reduced conflicts and better work quality. A study that was interested in the social effects of befriending depressed people showed that being in a better mood around depressed people helped them, however, a bad mood fortunately does not catch on so easily as a good mood.[34] In concrete terms, even though growing up in bad circumstances increases the likelihood of violence in an individual's life,[35] it is ultimately up to the individual to decide, whether to allow the environment to determine their future. In the end, our internal interpretation of the world determines how we see the world. Unfortunately, negative emotions and associated thoughts seem to be felt stronger than the corresponding positivity and associated peace of mind.[36]

Sometimes a collective mood can appear, seemingly arising suddenly out of nowhere. Primitive seizure of emotions can spread as panic, violence or rioting. The following study on this issue represents an example of collective micro-level mood arousal arationality. In Virgin Atlantic flight from London to Las Vegas, researchers analyzed fear reactions caused by turbulence affecting the passengers and how that feeling spread in the cabin. Even though there was no real danger on the flight, the collective feeling made most of the passengers very scared. While investigating the matter, some of the passengers claimed that one of the cabin crew had panicked, which, in turn, reflected on the passengers. However, none of the trained personnel on the flight had behaved unprofessionally. The conclusion was that people did not experience the situation as it really was, but primarily participated in the suddenly surfaced collective emotion.[37] The concept of a rational and thoughtful individual is fragile in panic situations – this is, of course, known and taken into account when training flight crew.

Another much-studied form of group behavior is stadium violence. Traditionally, football violence has been explained by the use of alcohol by men following the match, their low-level education or racist worldview. Recently these kinds of straightforward explanatory models that are based on completely exogenous causes have begun to be questioned.[38] It is true that football violence often involves the use of alcohol, low level of education (not always) and racism. However, these factors do not in themselves cause violence. Perhaps it would be fruitful to study the emotionality of the crowd before the match. Such emotional dynamics can already be fairly reliably predicted with AI technology that gathers the data from facial recognition and other biometrical systems. By analyzing the spectators' emotional state, it is possible also to identify potentially threatening or disruptive activity that might occur later.[39]

In recent years, individual psychological and small group studies have expanded to larger and larger datasets. In 2014 a research article published by Proceedings of the National Academy of Sciences of the United States of America (PNAS) showed through a massive ($N = 689,003$) experiment on Facebook that emotional states are transferred to others, leading people to experience the same emotions without their awareness. The effect was real without exposure to a friend and even in the complete absence of nonverbal cues.[40]

In Finland, a research project "citizens' mindscapes" 2001–2015 detected changes in social and national dynamics. Data was gathered from an Internet forum called suomi24 (Finland24), and it included 56 million messages that were categorized according to time, time of the day, month and year. Emotional words describing hopes and fears of 1.8 million people were mined.[41] According to the research, the happiness of Finns decreased steadily from 2001 to 2015, but at the same time the amount of concern has remained roughly unchanged. As for the days of the week, Thursday is the least happy day for Finns, perhaps, because that's when people pay their bills. However, on Saturday evenings after nine, Finns seem to be at their happiest. From two to four a.m., the discussion of fears and worries was strongest on the website. According to the researchers, daily, weekly and annual rhythms pertain to a very broad range of phenomena, which are yet to be fully explored.[42]

Since the data and study material of the University of Helsinki is freely available to all researchers, based on it, it would also be possible to carry out a socionomic analysis, comparing the variation of the moods with the OMX Helsinki stock index. This kind of research has been already done in the UK, as the following example shows.

The researchers[43] from Sweden, Spain, the UK and Denmark were able to identify significant associations between the local stock market index FTSE100 and UK residents' mood, as well as their alcohol intake and blood pressure. The findings were based on data spanning 14 years from a UK biobank ($N = 479,791$). In the study, results were adjusted for a large number of potential confounders, including age, sex, linear and nonlinear effects of time, research site, and other stock market indexes. Furthermore, the researchers found similar associations between FTSE100 and volumetric measures of affective brain regions in a subsample ($n = 39,755$; measurements performed over 5.5 years), which were particularly strong around phase transitions characterized by maximum volatility in the market. As the results confirm, phase transitions in society, indexed by the stock market, exhibit close relationships with human mood, health and the affective brain from an individual to population level. The result of the study provides evidence for self-organized criticality present in stock market behavior supporting the socionomic hypothesis of social mood as a driving factor in global societal processes.

As Robert Prechter has already written for decades, the social mood fluctuates and recurs regularly, and its changes are probabilistically predictable. With the help of big data, the digital humanities refine and renew our understanding of how the society works. Socionomics can make a substantial contribution to that research program. At the same time, the perception of individuality is challenged. The fact is that people are members of a herd and therefore follow the social mood. How much room there is for individuality is a good question to ask. As revolutionary as this sounds, the idea is not entirely new – the herd instinct has been used in modern advertising and PR for over a century.

Public opinion and public relations

The relationship between emotion and reason can be described as the relationship between an elephant and a rider sitting on its back. The elephant represents emotion and the rider on its back represents reason. In fact, if the elephant decides to go anywhere it likes, the rider, even though imagining that is in control of the situation, cannot do much. The same metaphor transferred to the relationship between the social mood and the individual is even stronger. If the elephant represents the social mood, the individual is the ant walking backward along the elephant's back. The core question for leaders and politicians throughout history has been how to control the societies they govern.

Although the question of crowds was already known in ancient Rome[44], modern literature on the subject emerged relatively late in the 19th century, first in Charles Mackay's book *Extraordinary Popular Delusions and the Madness of Crowds* (1841), then in Hippolyte Taine's *The Origins of Modern France* (1875). Mackay's book is a collection of stories of delusions, follies, such as crusades, witch hunts, duels and economic manias. Taine, however, tended to be more scientific as he was a great supporter of sociological positivism and one of the first practitioners of historical criticism, trying to find the historical reasons for the French Revolution. After these two pioneers, the book written by French physician and anthropologist Le Bon called *Psychologie des Foules* (1895) became the basic work of the field of crowd studies.

According to Le Bon, herd mentality as a feeling related to the power of the masses spreads in society as an epidemic, which leads people to either senseless violence or organized heroic sacrifice. The consciousness of the individual who joins the group becomes clouded and the ability to judge disappears, while the group forms its own collective soul. This collective soul is always more than just the sum of its parts. The totalitarian movements of the 20th century – Bolshevism, Fascism and National Socialism – exemplified Le Bon's desire for strong state power and the irrational nature of the masses. Among others, Adolf Hitler refers to Le Bon's theory in *Mein Kampf*.

In his book *Public Opinion* (1922), Walter Lippmann, the founder of modern media studies, describes people living in mass culture as a herd, whose control is necessary to preserve democracy. According to Lippmann, an individual's perception of the world is always empty and forms, in interaction with his interpretation framework, the so-called pseudo-environment. In this pseudo-environment, people behave reactively and impulsively as long as the prevailing and valid interpretation of reality is distorted enough, for one reason or another, which Lippmann calls "butting one's head against a stone wall".[45] A fanatic hardly changes his opinions, let alone his topics. Despite banging their heads against a stone wall, people still have a tendency to live

FIGURE 1.4   An advertisement from Lucky Strike campaign 1929[47]

more or less in their own (now maybe slightly changed) fiction, even after what happened, according to Lippmann.

Applying Walter Lippmann's ideas and having read Le Bon thoroughly, Sigmund Freud's nephew Edward Bernays (1891–1995), the "father of modern public relations", put into practice what his role model Le Bon and his colleague Lippmann had talked about. In his book *Propaganda* (1928), Bernays hypothesized that masses follow the herding instinct and thus, it would be possible to manipulate people's behavior without them even realizing it. To test his hypothesis, Bernays launched one of the most famous PR campaigns: the 1929 Easter parade in New York, featuring models with a "torch of freedom" Lucky Strike cigarette in their mouths. After the event, smoking, which was previously strictly forbidden for women, now took on a whole new meaning. Women's smoking became, not only socially acceptable, but also a sign of freedom and femininity. Under Bernays' leadership and guidance, the event was presented to the general public as "news".[46]

From a socionomic point of view, leaders and PR managers are powerless to shift the social mood. All they can do is capitalize on opportunities that the social mood trend presents. For instance, the Lucky Strike stunt at the 1929 parade came as a positive mood extreme was maturing, and the mood trend was entering a transition toward the negative. The PR stunt and subsequent ad campaign capitalized on the blurring of socially accepted gender roles that often accompany such phases of the social mood trend.

Regarding totalitarian regimes, a negative social mood opens a window of opportunity for such governments, as the negative social mood shatters society's desires for centrism and replaces it with polarization and a greater willingness to adopt extreme views. In this regard, the power of social mood and its sentiments should never be underestimated.

Notes

1 Frost & Prechter (1978); Prechter (1999a, 2003, 2016, 2017a and 2017b).
2 A more detailed presentation on phases of social mood in relation to Elliott wave patterns is found in Chapter 2.
3 Prechter (2016, 118–120).
4 Cushman (2020). Interestingly the article called "Rationalization is rational" and the followed commentary of it reveals how the debate of rationalization is rationalized by the researchers of psychology. The lack of role of emotions in the discussion is striking, not to mention that of mood.
5 Ketovuori and Lampert (2018).
6 Prechter (2016, 120).
7 Prechter (2016, 115).
8 Casti's depiction, recreated in Table 1.3, is from 2010. Today, socionomists would replace "rising," "peak," "declining" and "bottom" with "more positive," "positive extreme," "more negative," and "negative extreme," respectively.

9 Casti (2010, 25–26).
10 Prechter (2016, 375–376).
11 Prechter (2016, 111).
12 Scherer (2005).
13 Ekkekakis (2013, 5).
14 Alpert and Rosen (1990).
15 For a socionomic interpretation of subjectivity and objectivity, see Prechter (2016, 526–529).
16 Chapter 5's discussion on brain theory suggests that the percentages between emotion/reason might be 90/10.
17 Since existence precedes thinking, it is clear that thinking can be crystallized into a system by rationalization, which cannot be done in the same way for existence (that's what the arts are for).
18 Prechter (2016, 247).
19 Prechter (2016, 392).
20 Prechter (1999b).
21 Buckles, Hungerman et al. (2021).
22 Boler and Davis (2018).
23 Dernikos et al. (2020).
24 Guy and Mastracci (2018).
25 Gregg and Seigworth (2010).
26 Kenaan (2019).
27 Eisner (1985, 201–202).
28 Prechter (2016, 111).
29 Prechter (2016, 384).
30 Prechter (2016, 118–119).
31 Christakis and Fowler (2013).
32 Mueller and Abrutyn (2015). Socionomists would be interested to test whether there is an association between the background social mood and the incidence and magnitude of such suicide waves.
33 Barsade (2002).
34 Hill and House (2019). Socionomists would be interested to study if these results fluctuated with shifts in the background social mood of different eras and locations.
35 Huesmann (2018).
36 Baumeister et al. (2001).
37 Bruder, Fischer and Manstead (2014).
38 Patsantaras (2014).
39 Hutchins and Andrejevcic (2021).
40 Kramer, Guillory and Hancock (2014).
41 Lagus, Pantzar and Ruckenstein (2018).
42 Pantzar and Lammi (2017).
43 Lebedev et al. (2022).
44 O'Neill (2003).
45 …it may be a long time before there is any noticeable break in the texture of the fictitious world. But when the stimulus of the pseudo-fact results in action on things or other people, contradiction soon develops. Then comes the sensation of butting one's head against a stone wall, of learning by experience… (Lippmann 1947, 10).
46 Chakraborty (2014).
47 Stanford Research into the Impact of Tobacco Advertising (SRITA) https://tobacco.stanford.edu/cigarette/img44500/

References

Alpert, M. and Rosen, A. (1990) A semantic analysis of the various ways that the terms "affect," "emotion," and "mood" are used. *Journal of Communication Disorders, 23*, pp. 237–246.

Barsade, S.G. (2002) The ripple effect: emotional contagion and its influence on group behavior. *Administrative Science Quarterly, 47*(4), pp. 644–675. https://doi.org/10.2307/3094912

Baumeister, R.F., Bratslavsky, E., Finkenauer, C. and Vohs, K.D. (2001) Bad is stronger than good. *Review of General Psychology, 5*(4), pp. 323–370. https://doi.org/10.1037/1089-2680.5.4.323

Bernays, E. (1928) *Propaganda.* New York, NY: H. Liveright.

Boler, M. and Davis, E. (2018) The affective politics of the "post-truth" era: feeling rules and networked subjectivity. *Emotion, Space and Society, 27*, pp. 75–85. https://doi.org/10.1016/j.emospa.2018.03.002

Bruder, M., Fischer, A. and Manstead, A.S.R. (2014) Social appraisal as a cause of collective emotions. In: *Collective emotions: perspectives from psychology, philosophy, and sociology.* Edited by Christian von Scheve and Mikko Salmela. Oxford: Oxford University Press. pp. 141–155. https://doi.org/10.1093/acprof:oso/9780199659180.003.0010

Buckles, K., Hungerman, D. and Lugauer, S. (2021) Is fertility a leading economic indicator? *The Economic Journal, 131*, pp. 541–565, https://doi.org/10.1093/ej/ueaa068

Casti, J. (2010) *Mood matters: from rising skirt lengths to the collapse of world powers.* New York, NY: Copernicus Books.

Chakraborty, R. (2014) *Torches of freedom: how the world's first PR campaign came to be.* https://yourstory.com/2014/08/torches-of-freedom/amp

Comolli, L.C. and Vignoli, D. (2021) Spreading uncertainty, shrinking birth rates: a natural experiment for Italy. *European Sociological Review, 37*(4), pp. 555–570. https://doi.org/10.1093/esr/jcab001

Christakis, N.A. and Fowler, J.H. (2013) Social contagion theory: examining dynamic social networks and human behavior. *Statistics in Medicine, 32*(4), pp. 556–577. https://doi.org/10.1002/sim.5408

Cushman, F. (2020) Rationalization is rational. *Behavioral and Brain Sciences, 43*, e28: 1–59. https://doi.org/10.1017/S0140525X19001730

Dernikos, B.P., Lesko, N., McCall, S.D. and Niccolini, A.D. (2020) *Mapping the affective turn in education: theory, research, and pedagogies.* New York, NY: Routledge.

Ekkekakis, P. (2013) *The measurement of affect, mood, and emotion: a guide for health-behavioral research.* New York, NY: Cambridge University Press.

Frost, A.J. and Prechter, R. (1978) *Elliott wave principle: key to market behavior.* Gainesville, GA: New Classics Library.

Goodhart, C. and Pradhan, M. (2020). *The great demographic reversal: ageing societies, waning inequality, and an inflation revival.* London: Palgrave Macmillan.

Gregg, M. and Seigworth, G.J. (2010) *The affect theory reader.* Durham and London: Duke University Press.

Guy, M.E. and Mastracci, S.H. (2018) Making the affective turn: the importance of feelings in theory, praxis, and citizenship. *Administrative Theory & Praxis, 40*(4), pp. 281–288. https://doi.org/10.1080/10841806.2018.1485455

Hutchins, B. and Andrejevcic, M. (2021) Olympian surveillance: sports stadiums and the normalization of biometric monitoring. *International Journal of Communication, 15*(20), pp. 363–382. https://ijoc.org/index.php/ijoc/article/view/16377/3323

Hill, E.M. and House, T. (2019) Modelling the spread of mood. In: *Mood interdisciplinary perspectives, new theories*. Edited by Birgit Breidenbach and Thomas Docherty. New York, NY: Routledge. pp. 87–108.

Huesmann, L.R. (2018) An integrative theoretical understanding of aggression: a brief exposition. *Current Opinion in Psychology, 19*, pp. 119–124. https://doi.org/10.1016/j.copsyc.2017.04.015

James, W. (1950) *The principles of psychology, Vol. 1, 2*. New York, NY: Dover Publications. Unabridged and unaltered republication of the original 1890 Henry Holt and company version.

Kenaan, H. (2019) Changing moods. In: *Mood interdisciplinary perspectives, new theories*. Edited by Birgit Breidenbach and Thomas Docherty. New York, NY: Routledge. pp. 22–34.

Ketovuori, M. and Lampert, M. (2018) From 'Hard Rock Hallelujah' to 'Ukonhauta' in Nokialand: a socionomic perspective on the mood shift in Finland's popular music from 2006 to 2009. *Popular Music, 37*(2), pp. 237–252. https://doi.org/10.1017/S0261143018000065

Kramer, A.D.I., Guillory, J.E. and Hancock, J.T. (2014) Experimental evidence of massive-scale emotional contagion through social networks. *Proceedings of the National Academy of Sciences of the United States of America, 111*(24), pp. 8788–8790. https://doi.org/10.1073/pnas.1320040111

Lagus, K., Pantzar, M. and Ruckenstein, M. (2018) Kansallisen tunnemaiseman rakentuminen: pelon ja ilon rytmit verkkokeskusteluissa. *Kulutustutkimus.Nyt, 12*(1–2), pp. 62–83. http://www.kulutustutkimus.net/wp-content/uploads/2018/11/KTN_vol12_Lagus-Pantzar-and-Ruckenstein.pdf

Lampert, M. (2023) The Elliott wave model of social mood phases. *The Socionomist*, June 2023, pp. 3–4.

Le Bon, G. (1895/1995) *Crowds: a study of the popular mind*. London: Routledge.

Lebedev, A.V., Abé, C., Acar, K. et al. (2022) Large-scale societal dynamics are reflected in human mood and brain. *Scientific Reports, 12*, 4646. https://doi.org/10.1038/s41598-022-08569-3

Lillrank, P. (2021) Declining society and systems productivity. In: *Handbook of systems sciences*. Edited by G.S. Metcalf, K. Kijima and H. Deguchi. Singapore: Springer. https://doi.org/10.1007/978-981-15-0720-5_71

Lippmann, W. (1922/1947). *Public opinion*. New York, NY: The Free Press.

Mueller, A.S. and Abrutyn, S. (2015) Suicidal disclosures among friends: using social network data to understand suicide contagion. *Journal of Health and Social Behavior, 56*(1), pp. 131–148. https://doi.org/10.1177/0022146514568793

O'Neill, P. (2003) Going round in circles: popular speech in ancient rome. *Classical Antiquity, 22*(1), pp. 135–176. https://doi.org/10.1525/ca.2003.22.1.135

Pantzar, M. and Lammi, M. (2017) Towards a rhythm-sensitive data economy. In: *Digitalizing consumption: how devices shape consumer culture*. Edited by Frank Cochoy, Johan Hagberg, Niklas Sörum and Magdalena Petersson McIntyre. London: Routledge, pp. 41–58.

Prechter, R. (2017a) *Socionomic causality in politics*. Gainesville, GA: Socionomics Institute Press.

Prechter, R. (2017b) *Socionomic studies of society and culture*. Gainesville, GA: Socionomics Institute Press.

Prechter, R. (2016) *The socionomic theory of finance*. Gainesville, GA: Socionomics Institute Press.

Prechter, R. (2003) *Pioneering studies in socionomics*. Gainesville, GA: New Classics Library.

Prechter, R. (1999a) *The wave principle of human social behavior and the new science of socionomics*. Gainesville, GA: New Classics Library.

Prechter, R. (1999b) A socionomic view of demographic trends, or stocks & sex. *The Elliott Wave Theorist*. September 1999, p. 4.

Scherer, K.R. (2005) What are emotions? And how they can be measured? *Social Science Information, 44*, pp. 695–729.

Thompson, C. (2018) Stocks & sex: revisited. *The Socionomist*, June 2018, pp. 1–4.

2

ELLIOTT WAVE THEORY

After the Elliott Wave Principle is introduced, the chapter presents the history of the golden section. The regularities in nature seem to be reflected in the movements of the human mind, which, in turn, is reflected in the change of sentiments in the economy. The last part of the chapter discusses how the Socionomic Theory of Finance differs from other financial and macroeconomic theories, and to what extent they can be seen to complete each other.

On the first pages of Robert Prechter's book *The Wave Principle of Human Social Behavior and the New Science of Socionomics* (1999), the reader will find the following inscription: *This book is dedicated to Ralph Nelson Elliott, who deserves to be recognized as the father of modern social science.* In the 1930s, Elliott (1871–1948) discovered that price changes in stock market indexes produce a limited number of definable patterns robustly self-affine at different degrees or sizes, of a trend.

According to Prechter, Elliott's great insight was that financial markets have a specific organizational law of patterned self-similarity that is governed by the Fibonacci sequence, which ties markets to the laws of nature.[1] Such patterns may be used as a tool for market prediction. Elliott claimed that the wave pattern was an aggregate of "human emotions" which influenced developments in every field where human endeavor is registered, thus his model's descriptive and predictive capacities extend far beyond financial markets.[2] In short, Elliott's importance for socionomics is undeniable, while the basic principles of it are built on Elliott's work and observations.

Paradoxically, socionomic theory's relationship to Elliott is twofold. Although Elliott's observations regarding his Wave Principles are *de facto*, the starting point of socionomic theory and therefore everyone who studies it should know about them, application of Elliott wave patterns is not necessary for socionomic

DOI: 10.4324/9781003387237-3

analysis. Prechter himself states in his *Socionomic Theory of Finance* as follows: "Although [the Elliott Wave Principle] is an integral part of socionomic theory, one may investigate socionomic causality irrespective of the validity of the Wave Principle. If you are resolutely against it, ignore it".[3] In other words, socionomic thinking and analysis do not necessarily require understanding or application of Elliott's model, nor does the validity of socionomic causality hinge on the Wave Principle's validity. The Elliott Wave Principle and its use in stock trading is a time-consuming field in which to acquire expertise, but knowing how to apply it to market conditions is different from understanding its historical features or applying its principles to socionomic research.

The main principles of the Elliott Wave Principle are easy to understand. Usually, its basic pattern is introduced by considering a rising price scenario, such as the following:

- Wave one: the sentiment is overwhelmingly negative, but a few buyers emerge as the market starts to move up. This wave is marked by limited public participation.
- Wave two sees prices pull back in a corrective wave, but prices do not extend beyond the first wave's starting point. The background news is often quite negative, and it is common that some measures of sentiment even exceed those seen at the outset of wave one.
- Wave three is usually the most powerful wave. There is more positive news, and prices begin to rise steadily. Fundamentals, a lagging indicator, start to improve. Public and professional participation increases.
- Wave four is corrective and offers those who missed the early move an opportunity to buy the market on a pullback.
- Wave five is the last stage of the dominant trend. Mass psychology is increasingly positive reaching euphoric stage, and the market becomes overpriced. The public are heavy buyers of the market in this stage. The market is ripe for a trend change as the market becomes technically weaker while lagging fundamentals continue to look strong.

After the five-wave pattern that is called a "motive phase" the market turns to a downward "corrective phase" which takes a three-wave pattern in its simplest form. The corrective is illustrated in Figure 2.2 with waves A, B and C. Waves A and C move in the direction of the trend of one larger degree, wave (2), while wave B is a countertrend within the correction.

In the image above, the motive phase consists of five waves (waves 1, 2, 3, 4 and 5) that net advance and collectively form the first wave at the next-highest degree (wave 1). The corrective phase consists of three waves (waves A, B and C) that net decline and collectively form the second wave at the next-highest degree (wave 2). It is important to note that while the simplified charts in this chapter show all corrections unfolding in three waves, some

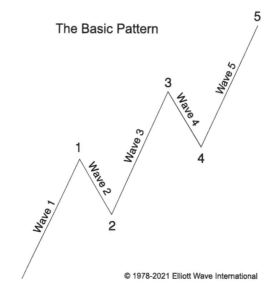

FIGURE 2.1 The five-wave pattern (Frost and Prechter 1978, 22).

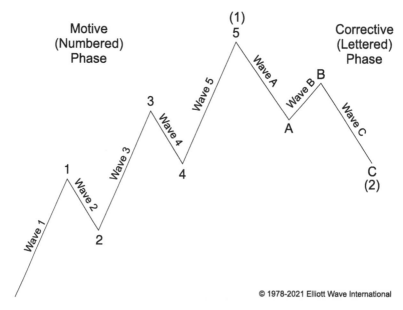

FIGURE 2.2 Motive and corrective phases (Frost and Prechter 1978, 23).

more complex corrective shapes also occur. It should also be noted that the wave pattern also works the other way around, when the higher degree trend in the motive phase is down, so is the five-wave sequence. In that case, the corrective phase works upwards.

Social Mood Phases Depicted on the Elliott Wave Model

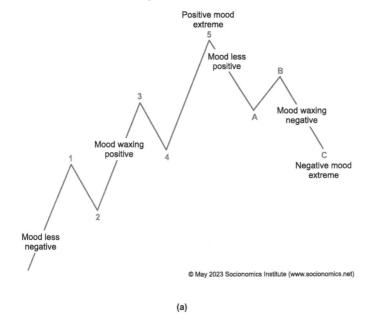

© May 2023 Socionomics Institute (www.socionomics.net)

(a)

Phases of Social Mood

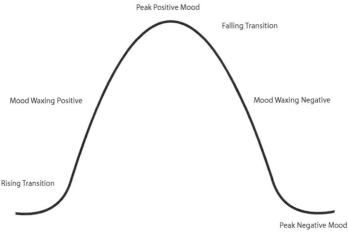

(b)

FIGURE 2.3   Social mood phases depicted on the Elliott Wave model (Lampert 2023, 3–4; in the latter panel Lampert presented a revised version of a figure originally published in Hayden, A. (2019). From your editor, *The Socionomist*, June 2019, 1).

Since in nature and phenomena, growth occurs before withering, it is natural to start examining the model through the rising trend before corrective downward trends. When we look at Figure 1.1 from Chapter 1, the Elliott wave model refines the former as depicted below:

The six phases of social mood from Chapter 1 correspond to Elliott waves following:

- Mood less negative: beginning of wave 1
- Mood waxing positive: middle of wave 3
- Positive mood extreme: peak of wave 5
- Mood less positive: beginning of wave A
- Mood waxing negative: middle of wave C
- Negative mood extreme: end of wave C

Elliott wave patterns can be recognized by following three basic rules:

1 Wave 2 always retraces less than 100% of wave 1.
2 Wave 3 cannot be the shortest of the three impulsive waves, namely waves 1, 3 and 5.
3 Wave 4 does not overlap with the price territory of wave 1.

From these rules, the essence of Elliott waves condensed into four principles:

- Progress is followed by regress.
- Motive waves subdivide into five waves of lower degree, whereas corrective waves subdivide into three waves of lower degree.
- A complete cycle consists of an eight-wave movement, which then becomes two subdivisions of the wave of the next higher degree.
- The time frame does not enter the pattern, so that the waves may be stretched or compressed along either the horizontal or the vertical axis without losing the underlying pattern.

Elliott did not speculate himself on why the market's essential form was five waves and three waves. According to Prechter, he just noticed that this pattern applies to the market. Prechter noted some mathematical principles that make a 5-3 structure a parsimonious form of fluctuation and progress:

> [T]he 5-3 pattern is the minimum requirement for, and therefore the most efficient method of, achieving both fluctuation and progress in linear movement. One wave does not allow fluctuation. The fewest subdivisions to create fluctuation is three waves. Three waves in both directions (absent arbitrary trend bias) do not allow progress. To progress in one direction despite fluctuation, movements in the main trend must be at least five

waves, simply to cover more ground than the three waves. While there could be more waves than that, the most efficient form of punctuated progress is 5-3, and nature typically follows the most efficient path.[4]

The Wave Principle is hierarchical as each wave has component waves and is itself a component of a larger wave, as shown in Figure 2.4. In other words, the same qualitative pattern recurs at all degrees.

Figure 2.5 continues the exercise to show waves at even more degrees: The scaling and repetition of the wave forms is what mathematicians today call fractality, although the term itself was not used by Elliott because it had not yet been coined. The term fractal came to the attention of the public in 1975 through the research done by Benoît Mandelbrot, whose mathematical approach resembles Elliott's empirical findings.[5]

The degree of a wave is determined by its position relative to component, adjacent and encompassing waves. Elliott himself named nine degrees of waves, from those that last for centuries, to those that last mere hours. In addition to original categories, Frost and Prechter presented 15 of them in 1978:

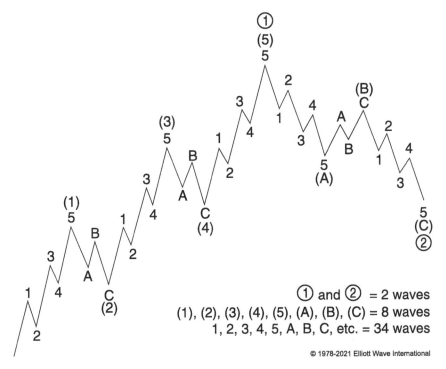

① and ② = 2 waves
(1), (2), (3), (4), (5), (A), (B), (C) = 8 waves
1, 2, 3, 4, 5, A, B, C, etc. = 34 waves

FIGURE 2.4 The fractality of the wave pattern (Frost and Prechter 1978, 24).

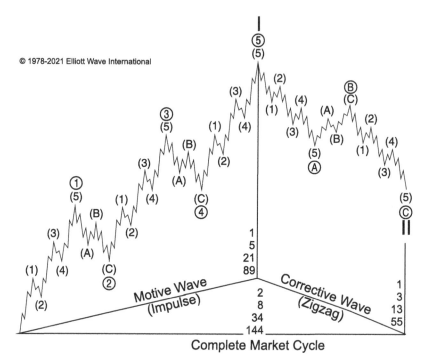

FIGURE 2.5 A market cycle at multiple degrees (Frost and Prechter 1978, 25).

There are no fixed time durations associated with each wave degree, as the Wave Principle's structure is based on qualitative form. But generally speaking, the smallest of these degrees – Minute, Minuette, Subminuette, Micro, Submicro and Miniscule – is mainly relevant for professional stock traders who follow markets intensely intraday. Today, the smallest degree waves are also relevant for superfast trading algorithms that execute intraday trades in milliseconds. Minor, Intermediate and Primary would be relevant to active traders as well as those who follow markets by reading newspapers and consuming financial television. When talking about waves of cycle degree, we are looking at waves whose trends are noticed even among the general public as they have a bearing on larger-degree trends in macroeconomic phenomena.

Degrees larger than these are, however, interesting from the perspectives of financial, macroeconomic and cultural history. In addition to the prices of stocks, bonds and economic indicators, the waves can be used also to predict such things as changes in values on the axis of anarchy/authoritarianism, births or, for example, the appearance of new inventions in history. In pessimistic times, new inventions can be related for example to weapon technology, while however, many positive inventions that have benefited humanity's enjoyment of life, are timed to more optimistic social mood.[6]

(↑ continue progression: upper case Roman/Arabic numerals; upper/lower case letters)

Wave Degree	5's With the Trend					3's Against the Trend		
1 Supermillennium	①	②	③	④	⑤	Ⓐ	Ⓑ	Ⓒ
2 Millennium	(1)	(2)	(3)	(4)	(5)	(A)	(B)	(C)
3 Submillennium	1	2	3	4	5	A	B	C
4 Grand Supercycle	Ⓘ	Ⓘ	Ⓘ	Ⓘ	Ⓥ	ⓐ	ⓑ	ⓒ
5 Supercycle	(I)	(II)	(III)	(IV)	(V)	(a)	(b)	(c)
6 Cycle	I	II	III	IV	V	a	b	c
7 Primary	①	②	③	④	⑤	Ⓐ	Ⓑ	Ⓒ
8 Intermediate	(1)	(2)	(3)	(4)	(5)	(A)	(B)	(C)
9 Minor	1	2	3	4	5	A	B	C
10 Minute	ⓘ	ⓘⓘ	ⓘⓘⓘ	ⓘⓥ	ⓥ	ⓐ	ⓑ	ⓒ
11 Minuette	(i)	(ii)	(iii)	(iv)	(v)	(a)	(b)	(c)
12 Subminuette	i	ii	iii	iv	v	a	b	c
13 Micro	①	②	③	④	⑤	Ⓐ	Ⓑ	Ⓒ
14 Submicro	(1)	(2)	(3)	(4)	(5)	(A)	(B)	(C)
15 Miniscule	1	2	3	4	5	A	B	C

(↓ continue progression: lower case Roman/Arabic numerals; upper/lower case letters)

FIGURE 2.6   Wave degrees with symbols (Frost and Prechter 1978, 27).

Even though the basic Elliott wave model is simple, the reality is of course, much more complicated. Elliott states that there are specific variations on the underlying theme, and he categorized those variations in detail. He noted that each pattern has identifiable rigidities as well as tendencies, or what Elliotticians today call rules and guidelines, which can aid wave identification.[7] For example, waves two and four usually differ in shape. If wave two is sharper, then wave four is often more sideways, and vice versa.

A more realistic Elliott wave might, for example, look like the below illustration from Prechter (1999). When the first iteration below is compared to the second and third iterations, the smaller-degree waves become visible and their fractality becomes more detailed.

A REALISTIC ELLIOTT WAVE

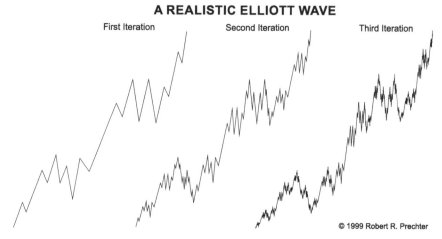

First Iteration   Second Iteration   Third Iteration

© 1999 Robert R. Prechter

FIGURE 2.7   A realistic Elliott Wave (Prechter 1999, 30).

From the rules and guidelines of Elliott wave formation, experienced traders can make probabilistic predictions about the future development of the market. A thorough understanding of Elliott waves is a skill that only comes from experience and the convergence of theoretical and practical understanding.[8]

The hypothesis that there are measurable changes in the collective social mood on which the prediction of the future can be made similarly to seismology. Although the methods of measuring the seismic waves of the earth have been developed, the prediction of the probable timing, location and intensity of earthquakes has not yet been perfected. Despite these shortcomings, the vulcanologists have been able to forecast and warn public of volcanic eruptions.[9]

In the same way, socionomics can be used in investigating the changes in the social mood. Of course, the wave theory has not convinced everyone. However, for those who are familiar with the cultural histories written by Oswald Spengler, Arnold Toynbee or Egon Friedell, this kind of idea is not unfamiliar or even strange. Would the Western science and enlightenment and the birth of modern society as a whole be a corollary to the long optimistic wave and related prevailing social mood? Indeed, moods have changed during the times and in different societies, for example, a positive mood preceded the Renaissance. To profoundly understand the concept of wave theory, the mathematical and natural scientific roots of socionomic theory must be examined in the light of cultural history.

Divina proportione

When R.N. Elliott discovered that financial prices form a fractal, he did not immediately notice the mathematics inherent in the Wave Principle. Elliott's publisher, Charles Collins, however realized that the Wave Principle was related to the Fibonacci sequence and shared his findings with Elliott, who quickly saw the connection between waves and the golden ratio. In 1940, Elliott came to the conclusion that the progress of waves has the same mathematical basis as many other phenomena of life.[10] The principle of human cultural fluctuation and progress is a phenomenon similar to the growth of plants, the flight of flocks of birds or, for example, the waves of the sea. These are all based on fractality and can be descripted with the Fibonacci number sequence.

The Fibonacci sequence of numbers was first introduced by Leonardo de Pisa, otherwise known as Fibonacci, in his book *Liber abaci* (Literally, *Book of the Abacus*) in 1202 and its revised edition in 1228. The book introduced Arabic (although originally Indian) numbers and proved the usefulness and practicality of their use compared to Roman numerals. The book provides among other things mathematical problems to its readers, which of the most famous is the following:

A certain man put a pair of rabbits in a place surrounded by a wall. How many pairs of rabbits can be produced from that pair in a year if it is supposed that every month each pair begets a new pair which from the second month becomes productive?

While in the beginning, there are just two rabbits, after a first month the first pair has produced another pair. In the second month the first pair has produced another pair, and now there are three pairs of rabbits, while in the third month the two pairs of the first month have produced two new pairs... and so on, creating the number sequence 1, 1, 2, 3, 5, 8, 13, 21, 34, 55, 89, 144, 233, 377. At the end of the year, there are 377 pairs.[11]

The ratio of the golden section, i.e., phi (Φ) (1+√ 5)/2 was suitable for the ratios of plant parts and tree branches. It is also the approximate ratio of successive numbers in the Fibonacci sequence, when the larger of the two numbers is divided by the smaller, More simply, the golden section can also be concretely defined with the help of the segments a and b, so that their ratio is equal to the ratio of the length to their sum:

$$\frac{a}{b} = \frac{a+b}{a}$$

The golden ratio is the infinite irrational number 1.618034... etc. However, the lengths of the line segments a and b are most commonly rounded as a ratio of 0.62 and 0.38.

As this number has many names such as "golden mean", "Divina proportion" its mathematical symbol phi Φ is derived succinctly after the architect Phidias, who designed the Parthenon in Rome.[12]

The golden ratio has been applied and studied by numerous artists and scientists[13] in different fields at different times, such as Aristotle, Goethe,

FIGURE 2.8   Mario Merz, Fibonacci Sequence 1–55, 1994. Turku, Finland.

Einstein and Le Corbusier. In music, *sectio aurea* appears at least in the productions of Béla Bartók, Jean Sibelius and Wolfgang Amadeus Mozart.[14]

In architecture, the golden ratio is also known based on the work *De architectura libri decem* from 25 BC by Vitruvius, the court architect of Emperor Augustus. According to Vitruvius, the three principles of architecture, beauty, durability and usability should guide the scale of buildings and the location of rooms. Leonardo da Vinci applied the observations of Vitruvius in a treatise on the proportions of the human body together with his friend and teacher Luca Pacioli in *Divina proportione* from 1509. For some reason, his famous Vitruvian Man is not, however, included in the book.[15] The drawing is certainly as famous as the Mona Lisa and the Last Supper:

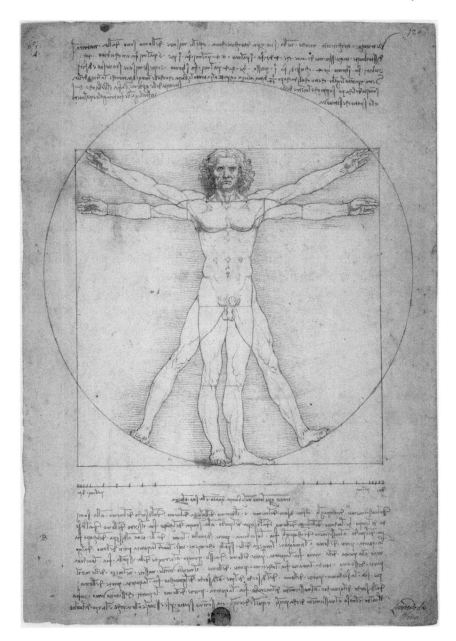

FIGURE 2.9   Vitruvian Man.

Since Leonardo's relationship with mathematics was more superficial than that of Pacioli's, he called the latter a master.[16] As a versatile Renaissance genius, Da Vinci had also many other areas of interests, and his shortcomings in mathematics do not detract from the overall value of his achievements. Although some of the proportions of the Vitruvian man are approximate (after all, the image represents an ideal man), it confirms the rule of the golden ratio through numerous observations, for example:

- If we take the pole point as the center of the human body and the distance between the person's feet and the pole point as the measurement unit, the height of the person corresponds to 1.618 measures.
- The distance from the fingertips to the wrist and from the wrist to the elbow is 1.618.
- The distance from shoulder level to the crown of the head and the size of the head is 1.618.
- The distance from the pole point to the crown of the head and from the shoulder level to the crown of the head is 1.618.
- The distance from the pole point to the knees and from the knees to the feet is 1.618.
- The distance from the tip of the chin to the tip of the upper lip and from the tip of the upper lip to the nostrils is 1.618.
- The distance from the tip of the chin to the upper line of the eyebrows and from the upper line of the eyebrows to the crown is 1.618, and so on…

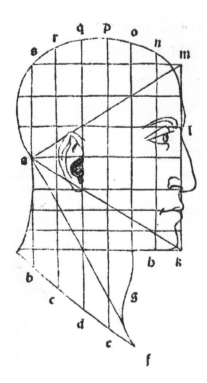

FIGURE 2.10 Divina proportione (Pacioli 1509/2014, 70).

In his work, Leonardo da Vinci did not yet distinguish between science and art, but saw both as ways to understand the principles of nature. The laws of nature were understood as given, but the ability to act on the basis of the conditions set by them, i.e., *Virtus operativa*, (i.e., practical reason and ability to operate), was understood as something that should be learned in addition to the things themselves. The word *Virtus* refers to virtues and operative action; nature should be approached, understood and ultimately utilized to build different things based on the observations.

Summa summarum, the relations in the human body seem to follow the law of the golden section. How then could one proceed from physical proportions to the movements of the human mind? In terms of the joint dynamics of natural science and mathematics, the analytical geometry invented by René Descartes in the 1620s proved to be a significant step forward. Descartes' geometry provided the basis for the work of Jacob Bernoulli (1655–1705), who invented probability calculation. He was enthusiastic about curves, differential and integral calculus. Based on these, Bernoulli discovered the so-called logarithmic spiral, which contained several amazing properties. It seemed to repeat its shape as it expanded, while this growth followed the principle of the golden ratio.

Spira mirabilis, the miraculous spiral, together with the words *Eadem mutata resurgo* – though I have changed, I rise again the same – was engraved on Bernoulli's tombstone – it's just a pity that the stone accidentally got an Archimedean spiral instead of a logarithmic one.[17]

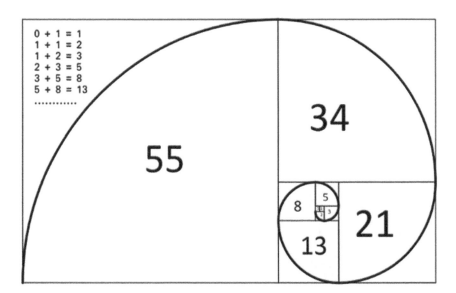

FIGURE 2.11 Logarithmic spiral (numbers represent the lengths of the sides of the respective shapes).

The ideas presented above were finally transferred from mathematics to biology around the beginning of the 20th century. In his seminal book *The Curves of Life; Being an Account of Spiral Formations and Their Application to Growth in Nature, to Science and to Art; with Special Reference to the Manuscripts of Leonardo da Vinci* (1914), Theodore Cook (1867–1928) went through 415 photographs of people, animals, architecture, art, flora, mollusks to pore animals, etc. He stated in his book that the spiral represents the pattern of life and the essence of its first principle, growth. The hypothesis by Theodore Cook was later proven to be correct, as the double helix of DNA was found by Francis Crick and James D. Watson in 1953. The structure of DNA is based on the golden ratio, as depicted in the following figure:

One can assume that this symmetry has a purpose. While it directs heredity, it also produces symmetrical life forms with a stable, purposeful and self-organizing structure. In a mathematical sense, one could talk about optimization. This self-organization enables growth, whether of a tree or of humanity, while all life phenomena follow their own inner purpose. The arc of development according to the golden ratio takes place in biology cyclically through alternating expansion and decay, growth and withering, from the

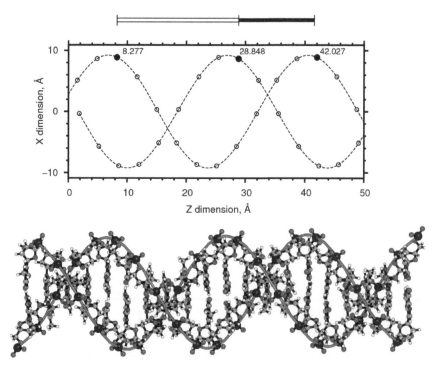

FIGURE 2.12 DNA structure and the Golden Ratio (Brain/mind bulletin, June 1987).

smallest cellular phenomena to galactic systems. Although we are part of nature, the Wave Principle of human social behavior is not only biological in nature but also fundamentally mathematical.[18]

By combining the movement of social sentiment, Elliott waves, with Bernoulli's spiral of logarithmic growth, we may see the phenomena in light of the cyclical nature of growth, flourishing and alternation. Of these, the waves represent mathematical variation – the growth spiral of biology:

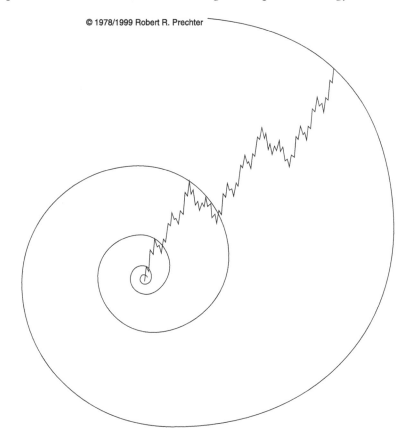

© 1978/1999 Robert R. Prechter

FIGURE 2.13   Spiral growth and Elliott waves (Frost and Prechter 1978, 125).

Figure 2.13, from Frost and Prechter (1978), shows that the peak of the five-wave growth cycle of the Elliott Wave Principle falls on the rim of a regularly expanding growth spiral. Specifically, the fifth wave peak of each successively larger degree terminates when it touches the rim of the spiral.

Fractal shapes are visible within organisms and in the creations of organisms, often on a larger scale than themselves, as we can see from the pair of images below:

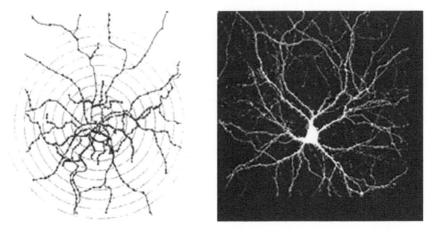

FIGURE 2.14   Greater Paris rail network (Stanley 1992, 2) and a nerve cell.

Fractal shapes, such as Elliott waves, are visible within organisms and in nature. The value of fractals is more than just purposefulness, efficiency, sustainability or other beneficial aspects – they are simply necessary for life itself.

According to Lipsitz and Goldenberger's (1992) study, both the complexity of the nervous system branches and the decrease in heartbeat complexity are associated with aging. In this case, the fractality of the body also decreases. It seems that complexity, unevenness and chaotic processes are related to the vitality of the organism. In other words, not only the efficiency and adaptability of a complex system but its very existence depends upon its fractal patterns of irregularity.[19] It is obvious to me that what is true for humans in this respect also applies to social super-organisms and societies, in particular. Excessive simplicity or one-sidedness is a sign of deteriorating society.

In his famous and much-cited work *The Psychology of Personal Constructs*, George Kelly (1955) states that attitudes and preconceptions serve as the basis of human decision-making. When examining neutral situations and related value claims with two answer options, negative and positive, Kelly imagined subjects' responses to be approximately 50/50. Objectively speaking, this seems logical. The experimental study showed that the distribution is, however, on average 62/38, i.e., in a slightly positive direction.

While the golden ratio as "the human factory settings" reflects the cognitive evaluation system built into a person, the bias inherent in it is seen as a change in society. It is also the source of Elliott waves,[20] while at the same time it works as "a hidden engine of history". Human imperfection, even if we might think so, is therefore not necessarily a fault – it can be part of a greater purpose. Of course, whether there is purpose and order in the world cannot be solved by the means of science, it is a matter of everyone's conviction and faith.

Since no further evidence shall be presented on this matter for the time being, the question of the truth of the above matters remains for the reader to decide. You may also state "we don't know" as an answer option. However, according to pragmatism's theory of truth, since utility is the essential marker of truth, socionomics must be tested for its functionality with its observations of human social behavior and the conclusions drawn from them. To do this, let's begin by clarifying socionomic claims about financial markets and the economy.

Sense and sensibility in finance and economics

Outside of socionomics, the orthodox view on financial market pricing relies on fundamental analysis that looks at companies' financial statements, while considering the company's future market potential. Under normal conditions at the markets, long-term index investing is taught to result in secure, if moderate, returns. Seeking better results than this, i.e., beating the index, is not possible all the time, and it also comes with its risks. The other broad type of financial market pricing analysis is a so-called technical analysis, which predicts the future of market prices by analyzing the form, shapes and movements of previous market price behavior. Factors of consideration include share price and price volatility.

Elliott wave analysis falls into the category of technical analysis. Socionomics in its turn is much broader, as it concerns itself with understanding the trajectories of trends throughout society and culture. Blending cultural and social psychological perspectives with financial analysis, the approach is both intuitive and holistic. However, how paradoxical this might sound, Prechter claims that socionomic thought is based on pure observations on reality, i.e., empirics. Based on the duality of metaphysical Wave Principle and empirical observations, I propose that socionomic theory can be classified as belonging to metaphysical realism. In metaphysical realism, the structure of the world exists independently of our thoughts or perceptions and is governed by natural laws that are fundamentally non-epistemic. In practice, this means that natural sciences are epistemic constructs describing the reality.

In other words, reality is not the same thing as the words and symbols, which are used to describe it. Even people are using words, the ontology of social mood is still primary and comes before the use of words, i.e., epistemology. Thus, the senses, not rationality, should be the starting point for observing reality. The following example of a typical five-minute period in the stock market reveals how metaphysical wave patterns manifest themselves in an empirical situation:

Let's say that there has been a bear market going on for a week. Now, to a pit trader, that's a major bear market: five straight trading days of declining prices, with small rallies along the way. It's already worn him out. One day, the traders are watching the tape, and it's kind of slow because volume has receded during the decline. Suddenly, the market seems to be stalled out. A couple of traders who have been there the longest, you know, the grizzled old guys that really know the game, who have been there for almost two whole years, are watching the tape from the back of the room, and they say, "buy me ten, buy me fifty, buy me a hundred".

A few heads turn because these are pretty good-sized lots. Sure enough, the market starts to tick up a little bit. Then it stops again and starts to recede very slowly. Most people are saying, " Ah, it's the same old stuff, a rally and a decline; it's going to come back to new lows just like it's been doing for a week. Forget it." They take another bite of their sandwiches and keep half an eye on the board. This is the point of lethargy and conviction that marks a second wave. Soon they notice that the market isn't making a new low; it's holding at a higher bottom. Well, to traders, that's a fundamental news event.

They start watching more closely, and all of a sudden, they get a bit excited, and one or two orders pop out. Then the floodgates open. They are screaming and yelling buy orders, and sure enough, prices are roaring up. It's a broad, powerful third wave. It goes on for a full minute and a half but ends abruptly, and another reaction sets in. Guys who bought late have a small loss. It is the fourth wave's "surprising disappointment."

Now, behind the scenes, over in the corner, there are some younger traders, who have been trading for only about week and a half. They have been keeping an eye on this action, saying to themselves, "Man, look at that wild move! Look at the money we could have made just then! If I'd only been long! I tell you what, if this market starts up again *one more time,* I'm gonna buy. I'm getting ready." They're watching closely, eyes riveted on the board. Sure enough, the market starts up again. Those young guys start to yell in their orders: "Buy me one! Buy me one!" The market jumps to a new high. Orders from Merrill Lynch finally make it down to the floor, ending as the fifth wave culminates. The old guys who started it all croak from the back, "Sell me ten, sell me fifty, sell me hundred," and the five-wave move is over.[21]

In this example, guided by the herding instinct, stock pricing follows the dynamic and constantly fluctuating social mood with its changing sentiments. Contrary to what is assumed in financial theory based on rational expectations, according to socionomics, share values are not based on companies' wealth, profit or other similar fundamentals. The radical conclusion from this is that stock indexes are not based on any real-world factor, but the current mood of the markets.

Prechter distinguishes between financial markets and economic markets.[22] In Prechter's "financial/economic dichotomy", financial markets are markets for investment items, whereas economic markets are markets for utilitarian goods and services. Supply and demand regulate prices in economic markets in the context of knowledge and certainty. The Law of Patterned Herding regulates prices in financial markets in a context of ignorance and uncertainty. In economic markets, prices are inversely related to the motivation to buy such that lower prices for economic goods and services result in more of them being bought (and vice versa). In financial markets, price and the motivation to buy generally go in the same direction, such that speculators have a greater desire to buy financial assets when their prices are rising and have a lesser desire to buy them when prices fall. Prechter points out how fallacious such behavior would seem in an economic market: imagine households buying less bread when its price fell or driving more when the price of gasoline doubled. In economic markets, participants consciously apply reason to maximize utility. In financial markets, speculators unconsciously apply the herding impulse to join the herd. The participants in economic markets are consumers and producers, whose opposing desires are mediated at the equilibrium price. The participants in financial markets are a single unopposed group of speculators whose spontaneous commands result in ceaseless dynamism in market prices. Figure 2.15 presents a more complete summary of differences between economic and financial markets at both the individual (micro) level and the aggregate (macro) level.

As Figure 2.15 indicates, Prechter proposes that the Efficient Market Hypothesis – one of the leading frameworks for understanding financial market pricing in scholarly finance – is applicable only to economic markets. His dichotomy also rejects the notion of self-correcting mean reversion in financial market pricing.

Prechter's financial/economic dichotomy is meant to describe two types of markets, each of which resides at a pole along a continuum of markets. In other words, in between financial markets and economic markets is a spectrum of intermediary markets in which utility maximization and the herd instinct work at least partly simultaneously.[23]

Prechter also posits that the market for the same good or service can alternate from being dominated by economic considerations to being dominated by financial considerations (and vice versa) based on the mental orientation of the market's participants. One example he gives is the housing market. In historical periods where the market for housing is dominated by the desire for the utilitarian consumption of "shelter", then housing will more closely resemble an economic market. When the mental orientation among participants flips such that the housing market is dominated by the desire to own "real estate" as an investment, then the housing market will more closely resemble a financial market – complete with pricing dynamism, speculation and booms and busts. In such circumstances, the more enthusiastic market participants are, the more real estate prices increase, eventually creating a

Per the Socionomic Theory of Finance (STF), Economics and Finance are Two Separate Fields

ECONOMICS
(Markets for Utilitarian Goods and Services)

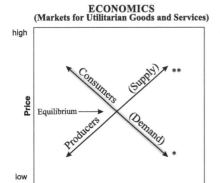

FINANCE
(Markets for Investment Items)

Features at the Individual (Micro) Level

Economics	Finance
Goal: Survival and Success	Goal: Survival and Success
Participants: Opposed Producers and Consumers	Participants: Unopposed Speculators
Orientation to One's Own Values	Orientation to Others' Future Actions
Independent Decisions	Dependent Decisions
Known present prices matter	Unknown future price changes matter
Context: Knowledge and Certainty	Context: Ignorance and Uncertainty
Mental State: Conscious	Mental State: Unconscious
Motivation: Maximize Utility	Motivation: Join the Herd
Means: Reason	Means: Impulse, Rationalization
Action: Considered Transactions	Action: Spontaneous Commands
Ultimate Result: Survival and Success	Ultimate Result: Losses and Failure

Features at the Aggregate (Macro) Level

Economics	Finance
Reliable Standards of Value	No Reliable Standards of Value
Rational Valuation	Pre-Rational, Impulsive Valuation
Objective Values	Subjective Values
Prices express information efficiently	Prices express mood and herding efficiently
Stability (Equilibrium and Mean Reversion)	Dynamism
Laws of Supply and Demand (S&D) regulate price	Law of Patterned Herding (LPH) regulates price
Motivation to buy moves in opposite direction from price	Price moves in same direction as motivation to buy
Price is a meaningful product	Price is a meaningless byproduct
Explanatory Hypothesis: Neoclassical Theory and the Efficient Market Hypothesis (EMH)	Explanatory Hypothesis: Socionomic Theory of Finance (STF)
Px Change Model: Statistically Random Responses to S&D	Price Change Model: Elliott Wave Principle
Product: Prosperity and Stability	Product: Boom and Bust at All Degrees
Benefit: Short Term Survival of Individuals and Societies	Benefit: Long Term Survival of the Species
Scholarly Domain: Economics	Scholarly Domain: Socionomics

FIGURE 2.15   The Financial/Economic Dichotomy (Prechter 2016, 247, which itself is a revised version of a figure originally published in Prechter
(2004). The financial/economic dichotomy. *The Elliott Wave Theorist*, April 2004, pp. 1–10).

price bubble that bursts when the mood of the market turns negative again.[24]
Similar tendencies are visible elsewhere. For example, during periods of eu-
phorically elevated social mood, the previous price records for art are exceeded time and time again at Sotheby's and Christie's auctions.[25] An extreme
in mood is responsible for extremes in speculative prices.

Scholars in behavioral finance and economics[26] have identified and categorized various heuristics and cognitive biases that cloud people's judgment in
financial decisions. Such sources of bias can include conformism (willingness
to consensus), lack of numeracy, wishful thinking, excessive trust in intuition,
etc. In his book *Thinking, Fast and Slow*, Daniel Kahneman[27] distinguishes
between the systems of intuition and the analytical human mind: system one
and system two. Of these, system one is fast, automatic and intuitive – system
two, however, is slow and logical.

According to Kahneman, intuitiveness and related biases most often lead
to wrong pricing in the market. It is worth noticing that Kahneman's claim
about "wrong" pricing is a typical behavioral claim. It assumes that there is
a correct price, but market participants get it wrong. According to socionomics, there is no correct or incorrect prices in financial markets, there's simply
the market price that the mood of the market commands in the moment.

Although behavioral finance and behavioral economics are interested in
non-rational decision-making in markets, just as socionomics is, their differences are thus obvious. Behavioral finance and behavioral economics see
financial market pricing as the outcome of a mix of rational processing of
information and non-rational psychological influences. In such a view, market prices are seen as generally rational with temporary anomalies that arise
when the non-rational mind gets in the way of market efficiency by mistakenly
mispricing assets. Socionomics, however, rejects the notion that aggregate
financial market prices are even remotely guided by the rational processing of information. Socionomics begins with the notion that such prices are
guided entirely by the non-rational psychological influence of social mood.
This non-rationality is not a mistake or a deviation from a "correct" price,
but rather a natural result of the expression of the human impulse to herd,
which is biological in nature.

In his book *Mean Markets and Lizard Brains*, Terry Burnham[28] states that
the thinking part of the human brain, the neocortex, is extremely vulnerable
to the limbic system, the area of the brain that regulates emotional life. Both
the non-rationality of financial markets and various addictions, from food to
sex, are connected to this same part of the brain. Guided by the herd instinct,
a person is almost unable to restrain himself, unless the thinking part of the
brain is able to prevent the impulses of the limbic system and the behavior
arising from them. Unlike socionomic theory, behavioral economics is far too
nice and tame to claim anything of the sort.

Both behavioral economics and socionomic theory challenge the Efficient
Market Hypothesis, the dominant model of financial market pricing in scholarly finance. When placing these three different approaches on a spectrum
in which aggregate financial market prices are seen to be fully rationally derived on one pole vs. fully non-rationally derived on the other, the Efficient
Market Hypothesis presented by Eugene Fama (1970) is at the rational extreme and Prechter's Socionomic Theory of Finance is at the non-rational

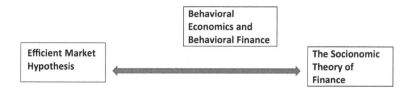

FIGURE 2.16 Rational and non-rational dichotomy in financial pricing theories.

extreme. Kahneman and behavioral economics, however, fall in the middle of the spectrum, as behavioralists propose that aggregate financial market pricing results from a mix of rational and non-rational influences. I think perhaps behavioral economics and behavioral finance are a little closer to the non-rational pole than they are to the rational one.

The Efficient Market Hypothesis and the Socionomic Theory of Finance are therefore opposite. The differences extend to metatheory. Wayne Parker argues that the Efficient Market Hypothesis is based on a worldview of mechanism, whereas socionomics is based on the worldviews of organicism and contextualism. According to Parker, it can be difficult for scholars to understand those who operate under a metatheoretical paradigm that differs from their own, which is why socionomists have taken great care to specify their metatheoretical position.[29,30]

Unlike the practical engineering sciences, economics is divided into many schools. They live side by side and use data from their own starting points. Since economics is a theory-oriented field by nature, its criteria are, however, like other sciences, cumulativeness, self-correction, falsifiability (that is, its claims should also be able to be proven false) and transparency. Prechter's position is that much of orthodox economic and financial theory is unfalsifiable but that socionomics is.[31] Because it is clear that such an argument may sound extreme, in the name of fairness it is also clear that Prechter's 800+ paged *The Socionomic Theory of Finance* provides the critical reader with details to understand, discuss and critique the theory in more detail. In my opinion, like so many other economic theories – from Marxism to modern monetary theory – the Socionomic Theory of Finance is a closed system that reflects its own principle ideas. However, in chapter 40 of *The Socionomic Theory of Finance*, Prechter introduces a rare insight: he employs socionomic theory to explain and anticipate shifts in the popularity of various financial and economic theories over time.[32]

The explanatory model goes like this: During periods of positive social mood, stock prices rise in the aggregate and the economy expands, while the belief in humanity's ability to rationally control the economy and financial markets prevails. However, during periods of negative social mood, stock prices fall in the aggregate, the economy slows or contracts, and the belief that humanity has little power over the non-rational and naturally cyclical

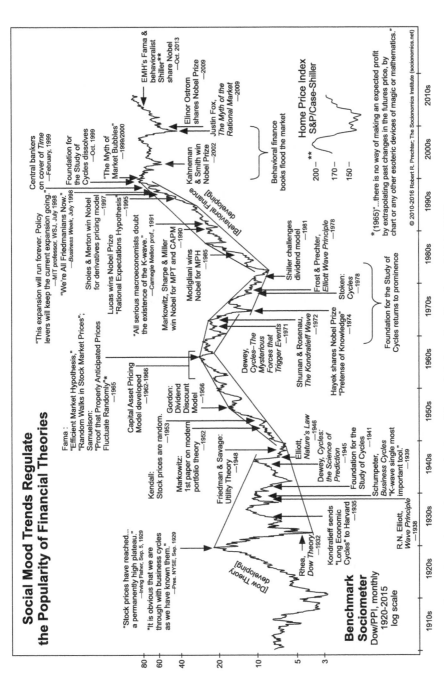

FIGURE 2.17 Social mood regulates the popularity of financial theories (Prechter 2016, 747).

financial markets and economy becomes popular. Thus, theories that empha-size rationality and human control over markets tend to gain in popularity when social mood is positive, and theories that emphasize non-rationality and the lack of human control over markets tend to gain in popularity when social mood is negative, as depicted in Figure 2.17.

According to Prechter, the history of financial theories, like other histories, comes in waves. In the picture above, he reviews a 100 years of economic and financial debate through the Nobel Prizes in economics, the birth of new economic theories, as well as significant anecdotes. Of the latter, consider the most famous statement of Irving Fisher, the most important representative of the neoclassical school, in which he stated that *"stock prices have reached 'what looks like a permanently high plateau.'"* The statement surely could not have gone more wrong, as he made it on the precipice of the 1929 crash and subsequent Great Depression. It wasn't until 25 years later that stock prices returned to their peak 1929 levels.

New cyclical theories, such as those presented by Kondratiev, Elliott and Dewey, came to the fore during the Depression. Yet as social mood grew more positive in the 1950s and early 1960s, popular economic theories again re-turned to an emphasis on rationality. Perhaps the most famous of these is the previously mentioned Eugene Fama's Efficient Market Hypothesis. According to the theory of this 'father of modern finance' and Nobel laureate, stocks reflect the ideal state of the market based on the best available information.

Whether it is the irony of history or its cyclicality, the recession of the 1970s challenged the claims of the Efficient Market Hypothesis just after it appeared. Socionomics proposes that the appearance of Efficient Mar-ket Hypothesis itself was a manifestation of positive social mood that re-flected a 24-year trend toward positive social mood reaching its extreme. From extremes in one direction, trends in the opposite direction naturally unfold – thus the market malaise and recession of the 1970s.

Notes

1 Prechter (1999, 6).
2 Elliott, R.N. (1938). The Wave Principle. Republished in Prechter (1980/2018), see p. 90.
3 Prechter (2016, 114).
4 Prechter (1999, 28).
5 Prechter (2016, 232). In my opinion, it is somewhat debatable whether Mandel-brot plagiarized his own theory from Elliott without citing him. As a proponent of the Efficient Market Hypothesis, Mandelbrot did not fully grasp the true es-sence and theoretical implications of Elliott's work or of market fractals generally. Nevertheless, before Mandelbrot's fame, nobody (except Elliott wave analysts and market technicians) had paid attention to fractality in financial markets.
6 Hall (2014).

7 Prechter (1999, 29–30).
8 This does not mean that a 100% accurate interpretation of all rules and guidelines is possible. Market analysis is always a matter of assessing probabilities. Furthermore, there are different opinions about the accuracy of the Elliott wave method in market forecasts.
9 Newhall and Punongbayan (1996).
10 Prechter (1999, 61).
11 Gies and Gies (1983, 77–79).
12 Prechter (1999, 61).
13 In particular, several American psychologists of the late 1800s and early 1900s, such as Lightner Witmer, Edward L. Thorndike, Robert S. Woodworth, and Robert M. Ogden, studied the psychology of aesthetics (Benjafield, 2010). According to Green (1995), the general tendency to dismiss the golden ratio as a "numerological fantasy" is an overly simplistic argument. There is evidence that people who are not familiar with the golden ratio find its ratios pleasant. The research question of the golden ratio is relevant for the field of psychology of aesthetics, and numerous studies have been conducted on the subject.
14 Whether they did this intentionally is a question of dispute. According to Phillips (2019, 424) the classical sonata form, which contains three parts that approximately can be measured through Phi, has probably affected the overall interpretation of its role in music. To apply classical ideals to all music does not, however, sound realistic.
15 Murtinho (2015).
16 Pisano (2016, 106).
17 Livio (2003, 116–117).
18 Prechter (1999, 83).
19 Prechter (1999, 188–189).
20 Prechter (1999, 206).
21 Prechter (1999, 220–221).
22 See Prechter and Parker (2007) and Chapters 12–15 in Prechter (2016).
23 Chapter 14 in Prechter (2016) presents an overview of intermediary markets.
24 Nobel Prize winners have begun to echo these ideas. In the second edition of his book Irrational Exuberance (2005), Robert Schiller warned of the 2008 housing price crash. His research on the matter dates back to the 1890s. Based on his team and colleague Karl Case's work, so called Case–Schiller index is used to measure housing prices.
25 Prechter (1990).
26 Behavioral finance is concerned with the way psychological and social factors affect decision making specifically in financial markets. Behavioral economics explores many of the same "non-rational" factors that can affect decision making in areas related to the broader economy.
27 Kahneman (2011).
28 Burnham (2005).
29 Prechter (2016, 621). For a fuller discussion of the metatheoretical foundation of socionomics, see Chapter 32 in Prechter (2016).
30 Parker's discussion in Chapter 32 of Prechter (2016) relies on Pepper's (1942) typology of four world hypotheses: organicism, mechanism, formism and contextualism. The lesser-known world hypothesis of selectivism is closest to my personal view: it is quite possible that even opposing theories can be right at the same time without their contradictions being essential.
31 Prechter (2016, 195–198).
32 Prechter (2016, 745–756).

References

Benjafield, J.G. (2010) The Golden section and American psychology, 1892–1938. *Journal of the History of the Behavioral Sciences, 46*(1), pp. 52–71.

Burnham, T. (2005) *Mean markets and lizard brains: how to profit from the new science of irrationality.* Hoboken, NJ: John Wiley & Sons.

Fama, E. F. (1970). Efficient capital markets: A review of theory and empirical work. *The Journal of Finance, 25*(2), pp. 383–417. https://doi.org/10.2307/2325486.

Frost, A.J. and Prechter, R. (1978) *Elliott wave principle—key to market behavior.* Gainesville, GA: New Classics Library.

Gies, J. and Gies, F. (1983) *Leonard of Pisa and the new mathematics of the middle ages.* Reprinted from original 1969 HarperCollins Publisher. Gainesville, GA. New Classic Library.

Green, C.D. (1995) All that glitters: a review of psychological research on the aesthetics of the golden section. *Perception, 24,* pp. 937–968.

Hall, A. (2014, December) Social mood influences technological development. *The Socionomist.* pp. 1–4.

Kahneman, D. (2011) *Thinking fast and slow.* New York: Farrar, Straus and Giroux.

Lampert, M. (2023, June) The Elliott wave model of social mood phases. *The Socionomist.* pp. 3–4.

Lipsitz, L. A. and Goldberger, A. L. (1992). Loss of 'complexity' and aging. Potential applications of fractals and chaos theory to senescence. *JAMA, 267*(13), pp. 1806–1809. PMID: 1482430.

Livio, M. (2003) *The golden ratio: the story of phi, the world's most astonishing number.* New York, NY: Broadway books.

Murtinho, V. (2015) Leonardo's Vitruvian Man drawing: a new interpretation looking at Leonardo's geometric constructions. *Nexus Network Journal, 17,* pp. 507–524. https://doi.org/10.1007/s00004-015-0247-7

Newhall, C.G. and Punongbayan, R.S. (1996) The Narrow margin of successful volcanic-risk mitigation. In: *Monitoring and mitigation of volcano hazards.* Berlin and Heidelberg: Springer. pp. 807–838. https://doi.org/10.1007/978-3-642-8008 7-0_25

Pacioli, L. and da Vinci, L. (2014) *De divina proportione (On the divine proportion):* facsimile in full colour of the original version of 1509. Leopold Publishing. http://issuu.com/s.c.williams-library/docs/de_divina_proportione

Parker, W.D. (2016) The metatheoretical foundation of Socionomics. In: Robert Prechter *The socionomic theory of finance.* Edited by Robert Prechter. Gainesville, GA: Socionomic Institute Press. pp. 621–-654.

Pepper, S. (1942) *World hypotheses: a study in evidence.* Berkeley, CA: University of California Press.

Phillips, M.E. (2019) Rethinking the role of the Golden Section in music and music scholarship. *Creativity Research Journal, 31*(4), pp. 419–427. https://doi.org/10.1 080/10400419.2019.1651243

Pisano, R. (2016) Details on the mathematical interplay between Leonardo da Vinci and Luca Pacioli. BSHM Bulletin: *Journal of the British Society for the History of Mathematics, 31*(2), pp. 104–111. https://doi.org/10.1080/17498430.2015.1091 969

Prechter, R. (2016) *The socionomic theory of finance.* Gainesville, GA: Socionomics Institute Press.

Prechter, R. (1999) *The wave principle of human social behavior and the new science of socionomics*. Gainesville, GA: New Classics Library.

Prechter, R. (1990, May) Art. *The Elliott wave theorist*, pp. 9–10.

Prechter, R. (1980/2018) *R.N. Elliott's masterworks*. Gainesville, GA: New Classics Library.

Prechter, R. and Parker, W.D. (2007) The financial/economic dichotomy in social behavioral dynamics: the socionomic perspective. *Journal of Behavioral Finance*, 8(2), pp. 84–108. https://doi.org/10.1080/15427560701381028

Shiller, R. (2005) *Irrational exuberance* (2nd ed.). Princeton, NJ: Princeton University Press.

Stanley, H.E. (1992) Fractal landscapes in physics and biology. *Physica A: Statistical Mechanics and its Applications, 186*(1–2), pp. 1–32. https://doi.org/10.1016/037 8-4371(92)90362-T

3

ON THE WAVES OF HISTORY

Generations come and generations go, but the earth remains forever. The sun rises and the sun sets, and hurries back to where it rises. The wind blows to the south and turns to the north; round and round it goes, ever returning on its course.

All streams flow into the sea, yet the sea is never full. To the place the streams come from, there they return again. All things are wearisome, more than one can say. The eye never has enough of seeing, nor the ear its fill of hearing.

What has been will be again, what has been done will be done again; there is nothing new under the sun.

Ecclesiastes 1:4–9

Charles J. Collins began his introduction to Frost and Prechter's (1978/2018) book, *Elliott Wave Principle*, with the above quote. Human immutability and the cyclical nature of history are key elements of socionomic theory when applied to human history and culture. The turning points in history are particularly interesting in this sense – the greatest historical peaks and achievements foreshadow the coming decline. The greatest setbacks, however, happen before regrowth. To quote the words of Edward Gibbon: history is really only a record of the crimes, follies and misfortunes of mankind. However, socionomics proposes that, despite setbacks, progress is the ultimate direction of history.

Gathering statistics on financial markets for the past 200 years is not particularly difficult.[1] There is enough economic data from the United States available for the research, all the way back to the early days of the Philadelphia (1790) and New York (1792) stock exchanges. The oldest European

DOI: 10.4324/9781003387237-4

stock exchanges Amsterdam (1602), Paris (1724), London (1801), Milan (1808), Frankfurt (1820) and Madrid (1831) also offer the same opportunity, although the majority of socionomic research to date has focused on the American market.

Studying long-term economic data is hardly the sole providence of socionomists. In the following graph, for instance, Bank of England researcher Paul Schmelzing depicts historical interest rate data from 1311 to 2018. As an aside, Schmelzing's work suggests that the interest rate had historically never been as low as it was in recent years.

By comparing daily prices in different eras, an interesting discovery emerges: stable prices, interest rates and valuation levels are fleeting. As the cliché goes, the only constant in history is change. Socionomists suggest a refinement: the only constant in history is *patterned* change. What causes the cyclical, patterned changes in history is a controversial question in economics, usually attributed to technological development. However, according to socionomics, patterns in financial market prices, macroeconomic fluctuations and indeed the histories of human societies generally exist because they are the result of patterned changes in social mood.

To perform Elliott wave analysis prior to the establishment of stock exchanges, Frost and Prechter (1978/2018) examined a dataset on prices for a "basket of human needs" compiled by Oxford University professors Henry Phelps Brown and Sheila Hopkins and enlarged by David Warsh back to the year 950 AD.[3] The shopping basket dataset has been used and studied by many other economists, including the famous Fernand Braudel and others. In subsequent research, Prechter took the analysis back even further into history beginning with the rise and fall of Rome by inferring the wave pattern from the tenor and character of recorded historical events.

The chart employs the Elliott wave labelling conventions from Frost and Prechter (1978/2018), which Figure 2.6 in this volume presents. The largest-degree waves on the chart are of Millennium degree. Their component waves are of Submillennium degree, and *their* component waves are of Grand Supercycle degree. As discussed in Chapter 2, the component waves link together to form the wave at the next-highest degree, thus creating a robust fractal pattern.

Differing from Edward Gibbon's famous Decline and the Fall of the Roman Empire interpretation, in which the heyday of Rome takes place between 90 and 180 AD, according to Robert Prechter, the peak of the ancient world took place already in 50 AD – just a few years after Rome had conquered Britain. For those familiar with socionomic theory, this interpretation does not cause a problem, because the slow decay of material prosperity, the weakening of the value of money or the disintegration of the imperial central power are only external later reflections of the social mood trend. Since Rome was not built in a day, also its decay was slow.

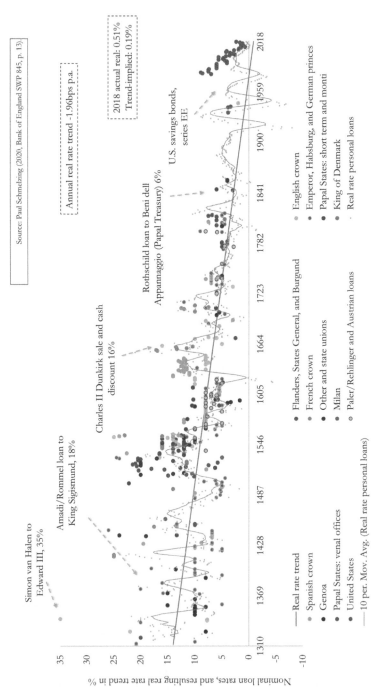

FIGURE 3.1 Eight centuries of global real rates, R-G, and the 'suprasecular' decline, 1311–2018 (Schmelzing,[2] 2020, 13).

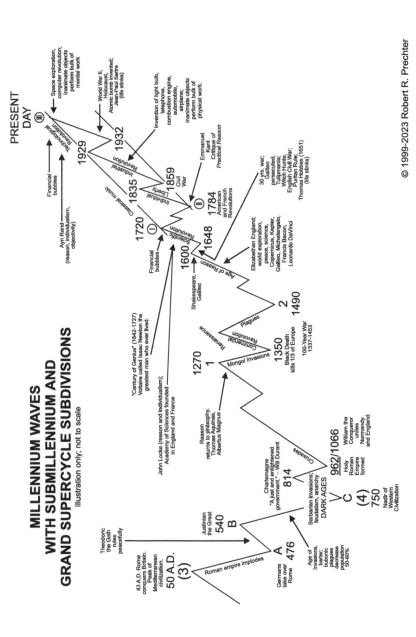

© 1999-2023 Robert R. Prechter

FIGURE 3.2 Millennium waves with Submillennium and Grand Supercycle subdivisions, based on Figure 18-7 in Prechter (1999) with an updated Elliott wave count from Prechter (2022); Elliott wave labels in the version of the chart presented here follow the labelling conventions from Figure 2.6 in this volume.

Following the peak of Rome, Prechter charts a Millennium-degree correction which consists of three Submillennium waves, the first of which saw the implosion of Rome and its conquering by Germans. The negative social mood was interrupted by a countertrend B wave from approximately 476 to 541, which saw the peaceful rule of Theodoric the Goth and the rise of Justinian the Great. But negative social mood returned and intensified as wave C unfolded from 540 to 750. One feature of this wave, and a hallmark trait of large-degree waves of negative social mood, was a series of epidemics and pandemics. The first of which, named after the emperor Justinian, appeared in 541 AD and raged from time to time in different parts of the Roman Empire for more than 150 years. According to possibly exaggerated claims, around 50–60% of the European population of that time would have perished from the disease.[4] The trough of Western civilization and the beginning of the early Middle Ages emerged by 750 AD, which marked a setback for scholarship and the search for new knowledge for hundreds of years.

At the beginning of the new Millennium degree trend toward positive social mood, mood is still depressed. It is simply a bit less depressed than it was at the preceding negative mood extreme. The Early Middle Ages ends with the so-called medieval commercial revolution of the years 950–1350.[5] During this period, the Holy Roman Empire is established in 962, and conditions in England change after the Battle of Hastings in 1066. The budding positive mood trend allows trade in conditions of peace, and the economy of the Middle Ages revives and organizes both in terms of professions and production (guilds and the Hanseatic League). A return to scholarship and philosophy forms as mood grows more positive still, which Thomas Aquinas expressed in his work *Summa theologiæ*, which he composed in the 1260s–1270s.

According to Prechter's analysis, another Submillennium degree trend toward negative social mood unfolded from 1270 to 1490. It consisted of three waves. The first of which saw the Mongol invasions, a plague once again – the Black Death – and the start of the Hundred Years' War between England and France. The correction's countertrend wave of more positive mood followed, which saw the Commercial Revolution and the Renaissance. The third and final wave of the correction saw the return of more intensely negative mood and another series of plagues.

However, the subsequent wave of positive social mood ushered in a period of economic reform that took place during the reign of Elizabeth I, England's first industrial revolution, the capitalist revolution, world exploration, and a blossoming in the arts and sciences with the eras of Copernicus, Kepler, Galileo, Da Vinci and Shakespeare. Modern financing begins in 1602, when the Amsterdam Stock Exchange is established.[6]

The subsequent trend toward negative social mood, which Prechter suggested lasted until approximately 1648, included the Thirty Years' War, witch hunts, Puritan rule, persecution of Galileo and the onset of the English Civil War.

The interest in the natural sciences that began in the Renaissance returned as social mood became more positive thereafter. This wave saw the "Century of Genius", which is crystallized in Isaac Newton's book *Philosophiæ Naturalis Principia Mathematica* (1687). Newton's work culminates the thinking of his era in the same way as Thomas Aquinas *Summa theologiæ* did in his own time. The wave of positive mood reached its extreme in 1720 with the height of an investment mania known as the South Sea Bubble.[7]

The bursting of the South Sea Bubble was among the first signs of a 64-year trend toward negative social mood. The wave of negative mood continued until into the 1780s and culminated with significant disruptions to the political status quo in the American and French Revolutions. The efforts of the reactionary British administration to limit the privileges of the colonies and to suppress their right to self-determination are typical of severe negative mood trends, as are authoritarian vs. anti-authoritarian conflict. However, from negative extremes in social mood, new trends toward positive mood begin. Modernization starting with the French Revolution of 1789 brought with it a period of rapid material development that has continued to our days on the back of a Grand Supercycle degree trend toward positive mood.

Moving on to the 19th and 20th centuries, Prechter's examination of history becomes more detailed and US-centric. The biggest countertrend waves toward negative mood within the larger-degree positive trend occur just prior to the U.S. Civil War and in concert with the great stock market crash of 1929. These events are tied to the U.S. context, but similar events occurred in Europe. For example, the unrest of Europe's Revolutions of 1848 happened during the same negative mood trend that precipitated the U.S. Civil War. And, of course, the outbreak of World War II in Europe followed the onset of the large-degree wave toward negative social mood that began in 1929 and persisted, by some measures, into the late 1940s. Other major events from Europe in the 19th and 20th centuries, such as the conditions after the Napoleonic Wars at the Congress of Vienna (1814–1815), the Franco-Prussian War (1870–1871), and even the consummation of the European Union can be contextualized using appropriate sociometers.

According to socionomics, trends toward positive social mood have brought life-improving inventions, progress and greater resources, while trends toward negative social mood have brought wars, epidemics and economic collapses. On the whole, the trends toward progress have outweighed the trends toward regress. The question, however, is, why can't we prevent negative social mood and its harmful consequences? Robert Prechter's answer deserves to be directly quoted:

> Who's we? You and I? What would we do? No one can change nature's physical laws, but a person can understand them and harness their power for his benefit. The same appears to be true of the laws of human social behavior.[8]

In other words, a person can only change himself, or at least try to. Changing the mood of society or the tide of history, however, is impossible. Of course, various would-be utopias have tried this with well-known consequences. Because utopias are both ahistorical and blind, the failures of past experiments are not remembered. George Santayana's statement[9]: *those who do not remember the past are condemned to repeat it*, is therefore true.

According to Prechter, the peak of the current Grand Supercycle wave will be followed by a strong corrective wave of commensurate degree, which will usher in a collapse in financial asset prices, a severe depression, social unrest and, later in the correction, wars. According to Prechter, if such a wave unfolds, stock prices could ultimately collapse by 90% at worst, bringing Western stock markets back to the level of the early 1930s. Naturally, this scenario sounds extreme, although it is entirely possible. At the time of the 2008 financial crisis, this risk became common knowledge. The biggest banks had to be bailed out because they claimed to be too big to fail.

In the late 1970s, Prechter predicted the large-degree wave of positive social mood that would come to the fore in the 1980s and continues today. Yet even at the time of his initial prediction of the boom, his view of the correction that would come afterwards in Western societies was already clear:

> As this century progresses, it becomes clearer that in order to satisfy the demands of some individuals and groups for the output of others, man, through the agency of the state, has begun to leech off that which he has created. He has not only mortgaged his present output, but he has mortgaged the output of future generations by eating the capital that took generations to accumulate.[10]

In the 21st century, countries have also started to live in debt like their citizens, and the end result is clear. At the moment, debt is only piling up as society hopes that so-called "helicopter money", i.e., printing money and more debt, would solve the debt problem. The saying "don't fight the Fed" contains the idea of the unlimited ability of central banks to regulate the market. Central banks do not, however, have such an ability. "Don't fight the waves" Prechter answers[11] – and when a Grand Supercycle degree wave of negative social mood unfolds, he predicts a deflationary depression will begin, and society ultimately will lose faith in monetary authorities. Only at this stage do many people realize how poor they really are.

In short, at such a juncture, the valid interpretation of reality will get a reframing that compares to Walter Lippmann's "head against a stone wall" mentioned in Chapter 1. However, a crash is followed by an upswing, just as surely as generations change and forget their previous experiences. The question whether the social mood is positive or negative makes a huge difference in our perceptions of other people and our willingness to cooperate with them, as Prechter states:

Major bear markets are accompanied by a reduction in the size of people's unit of allegiance, the group that they consider to be like themselves. At the peak, there is a perceived brotherhood of men and nations. ... In other words, at a peak, it's all "we"; everyone is a potential friend. At a bottom it's all "they"; everyone is a potential enemy. When times are good, tolerance is greater and boundaries weaker. When times are bad, intolerance for differences grows, and people build walls and fences to shut out those perceived to be different.[12]

In his 2016 article, "A developing reversal in the multi-decade trend toward globalization",[13] researcher Alan Hall from the Socionomics Institute referred to Prechter's writing above and described globalization as "the greatest level of human interconnectedness and trading activity in human history" which therefore may make it "history's grandest manifestation of positive social mood".[14] Hall then anticipated that the trend toward globalization would reverse as the large-degree trend toward positive social mood gave way to a corresponding large-degree trend toward negative social mood. Specifically, he predicted the following to emerge during a reversal in the trend toward globalization:

- Fear of foreigners increases.
- Borders tighten.
- Security and customs lines lengthen.
- International air travel suffers setbacks.
- Free trade policies roll back.
- New tariffs and other impediments to trade are introduced.
- International trade slows down.
- International businesses experience supply-chain disruptions, shipping problems and shortages of raw materials.
- Immigration policies tighten.
- Many of the foreign workers in the United States lose their jobs.
- Shortages of specific kinds of labor.
- International universities go under.
- Students studying abroad are sent home.
- International tourism declines;
- International stock markets and economies become less synchronized.
- Cross-border capital flows slow down.
- Protection becomes a growth industry, much as airport security has.
- Countries reduce international cooperation.
- Countries increase border conflicts.[15]

Many of the things in this list have already come true at the turn of the 2020s. It is almost impossible to find external reasons for all of this, even with humanity's tendency to rationalize. Therefore, two basic theses should be reiterated:

- According to socionomic theory, explanations of the aggregate tenor and character of social trends that rely on external (exogenous) supposed causes are, in fact, a posteriori rationalizations.
- Internal (endogenous) causes explain the aggregate tenor and character of social trends.

Hall calls the trend he anticipates "deglobalization". Deglobalization reflects the fear that negative social mood produces. How else do increased societal feelings of fear shape the course of history, according to socionomics? Next, we look at the rise of authoritarianism and then we explore a theory of historical memory and compare it with insights from socionomics.

Authoritarianism and democracy

The argument that political positions can be placed on a graph with two axes, and radicalism/conservatism (economics) and authoritarianism/democracy (individual freedoms) are based on Hans Eysenck's books *The Psychology of Politics* (1954) and *Sense and Nonsense in Psychology* (1957). The most interesting claims of Eysenck's theory include both the connection of personality traits and political beliefs, and especially the similarities between the extreme left and the extreme right. The former are violent anarchists, while the latter are violent conservatives.[16] Factors that unite these two groups include, among others authoritarianism, aggressiveness and dogmatism. Eysenck's research work was based on psychometric methods and factor analysis, which were widely used in the 1950s, in which he distinguished the R-factor radicalism-conservatism and the T-factor, which consisted of toughmindedness and tendermindedness. Eysenck describes toughmindedness with the words factual, hard, unempathetic, practical and unromantic, while the attributes of tendermindedness were words such as idealistic, soft, empathic, dogmatic and romantic.

Among social scientists with a positive attitude toward the Soviet Union, Eysenck's idea of equating communists with fascists was, of course, considered offensive. Both the Frankfurt School and the circles of left-wing researchers who were influential in Cambridge at the time strongly tried to question Eysenck's materials, methods and research conclusions.

Since Eysenck is one of the most cited researchers of his time, his model has served as a role model for many other similar matrices in the social sciences. One such matrix that socionomists have used was created by David Nolan (1971). The classic iteration of the so-called Nolan Chart depicts political space using a vertical axis with extremes of "Libertarian" and "Authoritarian", a horizontal axis with extremes of "Liberal" and "Conservative", and a "Centrist" area in the middle.

Socionomist Alan Hall adapted Nolan's map of the political landscape to show a Centrist inner diamond with a vertical "Libertarian" to "Populist" axis and a horizontal "Liberal" to "Conservative" axis, and a more-extreme outer diamond with a vertical "Anarchist" to "Authoritarian/Totalitarian" axis and a horizontal "Far Left" to "Far Right" axis.[17] This depiction, which Hall called the Socionomic Nolan Chart, is shown in Figure 3.3.

As depicted in the figure, Hall noted that in times when social mood is positive, a society's political status quo is likely to reside somewhere within the Centrist inner diamond. In times when social mood is quite negative, however, a society's politics is likely to fracture, with clusters of competing factions forming in the more-extreme outer diamond.

Hall's depiction further illustrates dynamic movement in the political status quo as positive and negative mood trends unfold. In Figures 3.4–3.9, Hall illustrates how society's bounds of political normalcy and consensus shift as social mood fluctuates from a positive mood extreme to a negative mood extreme and then back again.

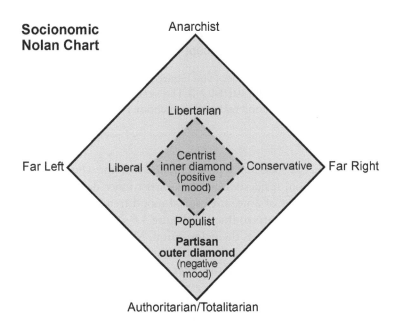

FIGURE 3.3 Socionomic Nolan Chart (Hall, 2010a, 2).

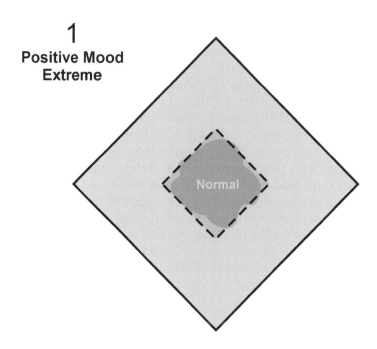

1
Positive Mood
Extreme

© Socionomics Institute (www.socionomics.net)
Four-point diamond concept courtesy of David Nolan

FIGURE 3.4 Positive mood extreme. (The Figure is based on an image originally published in Hall (2010a, 2).) The version shown here is from Hall (2017). Social mood regulates perceptions of political normality. Prechter (2017b).

Figure 3.4 depicts a society at a positive mood extreme whose political consensus, for illustration, resides within the centrist inner diamond. Figure 3.5 shows that at the onset of a negative social mood trend, polarization begins and political consensus starts to fracture. Figure 3.6 shows that as the negative mood trend intensifies, so does the polarization. More extreme points of view attract adherents. By the negative mood extreme, factions of society cluster nearer to the extreme positions on the outer diamond, as shown in Figure 3.7. The factions compete for dominance, and eventually one group wins. As the new positive mood trend begins to unfold, as shown in Figure 3.8, a consensus reforms around the location of the winning faction. As the figure suggests, we do not know which faction will win ahead of time, but it is likely that the "new normal" that forms will be in a different location than was the political consensus that held sway at the prior positive mood extreme. As positive mood intensifies, the political consensus moves closer to the center, as shown in Figure 3.9.

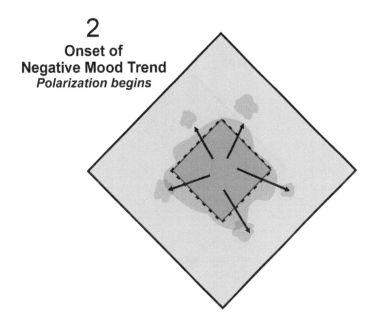

© Socionomics Institute (www.socionomics.net)
Four-point diamond concept courtesy of David Nolan

FIGURE 3.5   Onset of negative mood trend: Polarization begins. (The Figure is based on an image originally published in Hall (2010a, 2).) The version shown here is from Hall (2017). Social mood regulates perceptions of political normality. Prechter (2017b).

As an example of the more-extreme views that have come to the fore in recent negative mood trends, Hall lists the Occupy Wall Street and Tea Party movements, which emerged during the same negative social mood trend that produced the Global Financial Crisis.[18]

Hall (2010a, 2010b) uses the Socionomic Nolan Chart to understand the periodic rise of the social embrace of authoritarianism. Severe negative mood trends do not guarantee that society will embrace authoritarianism. But the fracturing of centrist consensus during such periods opens the door for the social embrace of more extreme views, of which authoritarianism is one possibility. Negative social mood trends often see authoritarian vs. anti-authoritarian conflict. Sometimes the authoritarians win, other times, such as in the American Revolution, the anti-authoritarians gain the upper hand.

Ethnocentrism, i.e., identification with the world view of one's own reference group, and associated dogmatism come to the fore as society polarizes, which makes it unlikely that anyone could or would even want to change

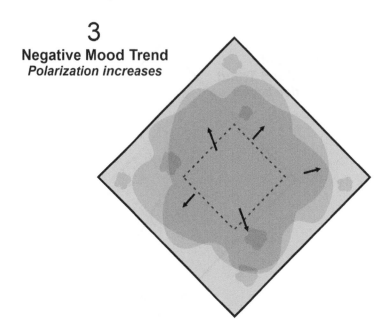

3
Negative Mood Trend
Polarization increases

© Socionomics Institute (www.socionomics.net)
Four-point diamond concept courtesy of David Nolan

FIGURE 3.6   Negative mood trend: Polarization increases. (The Figure is based on
an image originally published in Hall (2010a, 2).) The version shown
here is from Hall (2017). Social mood regulates perceptions of political normality. Prechter (2017b).

their mind based on evidence or logic. Hall (2010b, 1) notes that authoritarianism expert Robert Altemeyer has identified that authoritarian followers
are more prone to feeling afraid than most people. Heightened societal fear is
a hallmark of a deeply negative social mood trend.

Although the content of authoritarian regimes certainly varies according
to the historical situation, their forms are not essentially different, whatever
their ideological starting points. As the negative social mood intensifies, the
longing for a strong state power – a longing which arose from people's mood-
induced fears – can likewise intensify. From here, Hall (2010b) describes the
development process:

> As society's consensus diffuses into fearful discord, authoritarianism gains
> footholds. The majority of people see each authoritarian step as merely
> temporary, necessary inconveniences—small freedoms traded for prom-
> ises of safety. As fear increases, society makes ever-larger concessions.

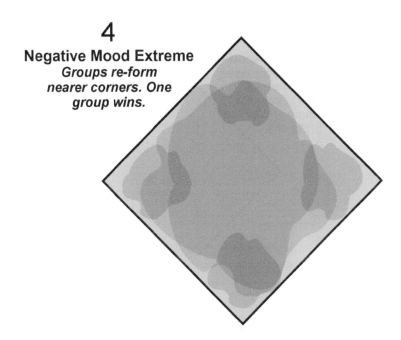

4
Negative Mood Extreme
Groups re-form nearer corners. One group wins.

© Socionomics Institute (www.socionomics.net)
Four-point diamond concept courtesy of David Nolan

FIGURE 3.7 Negative mood extreme: Groups re-form nearer corners. One group wins. (The Figure is based on an image originally published in Hall (2010a, 2).) The version shown here is from Hall (2017). Social mood regulates perceptions of political normality. Prechter (2017b).

If a negative trend in social mood is large enough, blatantly authoritarian leaders emerge and promise security. They attract support as well as strident opposition.

(2)

Among the social manifestations that may occur under a "new normal" of socially accepted authoritarianism are freedom-curtailing legislation and related speech codes. Something akin to Orwellian newspeak may arise and represent an extreme form of rationalization. Perhaps so-called thought crimes will be punished. Anti-authoritarians and citizens who have suffered the most from the measures of those in power may begin to reorganize and start resistance. Correspondingly, those in power may tighten their grip and crack down on dissent.

To maintain their power, governments have at their disposal numerous means to tame the opposition. Under the guise of combatting an external

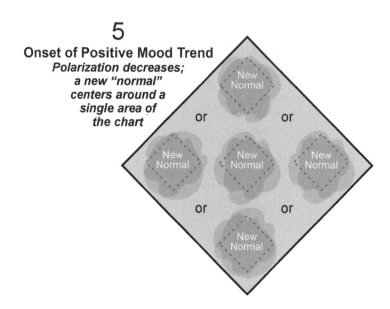

5

Onset of Positive Mood Trend
*Polarization decreases;
a new "normal"
centers around a
single area of
the chart*

© Socionomics Institute (www.socionomics.net)
Four-point diamond concept courtesy of David Nolan

FIGURE 3.8   Onset of positive mood trend: Polarization decreases; a new "normal" centers around a single area of the chart. (The Figure is based on an image originally published in Hall (2010a, 2).) The version shown here is from Hall (2017). Social mood regulates perceptions of political normality. Prechter (2017b).

enemy or internal threats, some internet functions can be closed, or their contents censored, be it discussion forums, comment sections or social media channels. Prohibitions related to the activities of unwanted organizations, political movements or people's movements are also an effective way to limit civic activities. Elections can also be moved or manipulated. The imposition of economic sanctions and new taxes, as well as restrictions on business activities, are all also means by which an authoritarian regime can seek to control the public. New forms of technological supervision may be tested and introduced. Violent demonstrations and the tightening grip of the police may be seen more and more often.

However, even the most strident authoritarian regimes have relaxed their grip to some degree as social mood became more positive. Ultimately social mood has authority over even the authoritarians.

Prechter (1999, 259) says the stock market is like a thermometer with respect to social mood, and it is like a barometer with respect to public action. As Chapter 1 in this volume discussed, a socionomist can track the transition

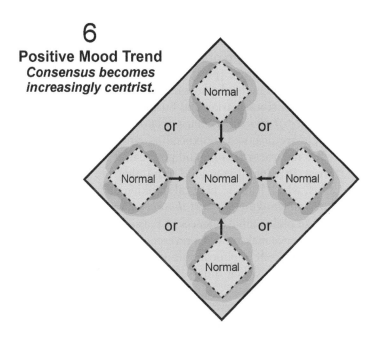

6
Positive Mood Trend
Consensus becomes increasingly centrist.

© Socionomics Institute (www.socionomics.net)
Four-point diamond concept courtesy of David Nolan

FIGURE 3.9   Positive mood trend: Consensus becomes increasingly centrist. (The Figure is based on an image originally published in Hall (2010a, 2).) The version shown here is from Hall (2017). Social mood regulates perceptions of political normality. Prechter (2017b).

from positive to negative mood (and vice versa) by studying the relative frequency and intensity of positive vs. negative mood expressions. The following quote from Prechter (1999, 229–230) gives some examples:

1   *Concord/Discord*: A [positive] mood leads to a substantial consensus in politics, culture and social vision; a [negative] mood leads to a divided, radical climate. After the social mood has [trended toward the positive] for a number of years, the society tends to be peaceful; after it has [trended toward the negative] for a number of years, it tends to become involved in wars.

2   *Inclusion/Exclusion*: A [positive] mood leads to feelings of social brotherhood and acceptance among races, religions and political territories, as well as toward animals, plants and proposed aliens. A [negative] mood leads to apartheid, religious animosity, cavalier cruelty, secession, independence movements and images of aliens as monsters.

3 *Forbearance/Anger*: A [positive] mood leads to social expressions of acquiescence, apology and tolerance. A [negative] mood leads to social expressions of resistance, recrimination and intolerance.

4 *Confidence/Fear*: A [positive] mood leads to speculation in the stock market and in business. A [negative] mood causes risk aversion in the stock market and business.

5 *Embrace of effort/Avoidance of effort*: In a [positive] mood trend, people are disposed to expending effort, both mental, which elevates the use of reason, and physical, which elevates the ideal of fitness. In a [negative] mood trend, they are disposed to avoiding effort, which leads to magical thinking and physical laziness.

6 *Practical thinking/Magical thinking*: Practical thinking manifests itself in philosophic defences of reason, self-providence, individualism, peace making and a reverence for science. Magical thinking manifests itself in philosophic attacks on reason, self-abnegation, collectivism, which hunts, war-making and a reverence for religion.

7 *Constructiveness/Destructiveness*: The impulse to build shows up in construction of record-breaking skyscraper buildings at [positive social mood extremes]. At [negative social mood extremes], few buildings are built, and many of those already in place may be burned or bombed out of existence.

8 *Desiring power over nature/Desiring power over people*: Desiring power over nature leads to a naturalistic mindset, political freedom and peaceful technological advances. Desiring power over people leads to a socialistic mindset, political repression and technological advances in waring.[19]

Prechter argues that humans are naturally inclined to create and change. This tendency is so strong that it does not depend on how good or bad the change may be. In the aggregate, the tenor and character of such changes depend only on social mood. He says that it seems human nature has within it the seeds of social trends and social change. As Prechter (1999, 230) writes, "adversity eventually breeds a desire to take responsibility, achieve and succeed, while prosperity eventually breeds irresponsibility, complacency and sloth".

As a member of a herd and influenced by the social mood, an individual has very limited opportunities to influence the kind of society and conditions they live in. The choice is between authoritarianism and democracy. Unfortunately, it is possible only for individuals to develop an ability to deviate from the social mood trend, while society as a whole is beholden to it.

In principle, my view is that social decision-making must always be balanced according to the *checks and balances*, where different actors have the authority to prevent other actors' decisions and excesses, if necessary.

However, since the social mood of the masses cannot be controlled or even directed according to socionomics, there is actually very little a society can do to prevent the societal and political consequences of the social mood trend from manifesting. Yet recall that a large-degree negative social mood trend does not demand authoritarianism, only disruptions to the political status quo. Among those potential disruptions are conflicts between authoritarians and anti-authoritarians. For those who would prefer to see one side win over the other, a negative mood trend presents a window of opportunity to act to make it so.

Although there has been no major change in the number of democratic countries so far, according to the *Freedom in the World 2020* report, social development within nations has been negative for 14 years in a row from the perspectives of freedom of speech, religion, association and assembly.[20] According to the same organization's recent report on internet freedom, at least 55 national authorities investigate, arrest or convict people because of the opinions they express on social media. According to socionomics, these anti-democratic winds are likely to gust even harder when social mood grows more negative. The question is as follows: Will any anti-authoritarian movements rise up to challenge them?

A complementary view: society and its memories

Unlike many other historical theories, socionomic theory suggests that history does not consist primarily of the actions of people or the stories they tell about these events. According to socionomics, the former are reflections and references of prevalent social mood and the latter are their rationalizations. These rationalizations (narrations) are repeated over and over again, even if their veracity may not be true. Because shared stories reflect a collective feeling, I propose that they contain also emotional meanings that are visible in culture.

In my view, culture determines people's way of being, people's everyday life, clothing, habitus and ultimately it comes visible also in the works of art, music, architecture and cultural environments. The more people are committed to the local culture and define their identity through it, the less it becomes questioned. Culture, as a deeper concept than identity, is a longer cycle phenomenon than shorter and changing identities. Identities take a stand on the prevailing conditions of a culture, either by trying to change things or by adopting the values and perceptions of the former. Together these two form "environmental niches"[21] that provide a safe context for symbols and traditions to become, as an integral part of how an individual understands his own existence.[22] Since culture is a belief system that is based on mood, the change in cultures happens, only through a systemic transition in social mood.[23] In other words, when systemic change happens the doubt gives birth to a new search of meanings and discoveries. Substantial change and the arrival of a new era will come when the shift in mood is large enough.

The idea that most major historical events have always been preceded by some kind of mood change is obvious among many scholars of cultural history. For example, the *French Annales School* studies intellectual frameworks and interpretations in which historical patterns are identified. According to the *Annalists*, historical events are secondary to the mental frameworks that can be approached by identifying patterns in social, economic, statistical or, for example, medical reports. In the *Annales* tradition, historical rationality and emphasis on individual action are replaced by human will, which can be understood by studying the collective elements of human consciousness.[24] Although the French school and socionomics resemble each other, there are no direct connections between them. What they have in common is that the prevailing atmosphere in society "tunes" and sets the events that can be analyzed through a serial study of data, such as prices.

However, for both of the schools, the question of how mood transmissions in human populations occur is still a challenge. While some historians of the *Annales* place more emphasis on *mentalities*, others place more emphasis on the social structures that set limits to people's living conditions in a given era. Socionomics, however, refers unequivocally to social mood, proposes that mood naturally arises rather than being transmitted from one generation to another. It rejects the notion of generations altogether as a means of demarcating boundaries between cultural eras, proposing instead that substantial shifts in society and culture occur when there are significant shifts in social mood. However, this absolute idealism, in which society is deterministically subordinate to the social mood, requires a closer examination and perhaps can be better understood by comparing it to a research paradigm that aims to account for the transmission of cultural feelings and stories. One research approach that deals with the latter kind of question is called mnemohistory.[25]

Unlike mainstream historical research, mnemohistory is interested in how historic events manifest specific situations and how they are translated over time and actualized in new historical settings. The central questions for mnemohistory are as follows: What is known of the past in the present? Why is it that some versions of the past triumph, while others fail? Which events or other phenomena from the past are selected and how are they represented? How is the past used in order to legitimize or explain the happenings in the present? Why do people prefer one image of the past over another?[26]

Let's consider these questions through two historical examples. The two last great famines during the peace-time in the 19th-century Europe, which occurred in Finland and Ireland, offer us a useful pair of case studies. In the period 1865–1869 Finland lost 10–12% of its population (approximately 250,000 deaths), while in Ireland in 1845–1852 the population decreased by around 15–20% (approximately one million deaths that combined with famine-related emigration and decreased fertility).[27] Since both countries had a large rural population dependent on one-sided and vulnerable agriculture, in Ireland potato and in Finland rye, historians typically identify the primary and triggering cause of the famines as crop failure. In Ireland, potato blight (*Phytophthora infestans*) destroyed the potato crop both in 1845 and 1846, while occurring again in 1848 and in a smaller scale in the early 1850s. In Finland, abnormal weather conditions throughout 1860s cut the production of rye in several consecutive years, while 1867 had the worst of these years' May mean temperatures over large areas of Northern Europe.[28]

Another factor that clearly affected the situation in both Ireland and Finland had similar features as being proto-states of larger British and Russian empires. It meant that the countries did not have full control of their economy nor policy that would have been used for vigorous fight against the hunger. Instead of taking care of their citizens, in Finland, 33,000 unmilled grain barrels were shipped out from the country even though people were starving.[29] The same happened also in Ireland nine years earlier[30]:

Almost 4,000 vessels carried food from Ireland to the ports of Bristol, Glasgow, Liverpool and London during 1847, when 400,000 Irish men, women and children died of starvation and related diseases. The food was shipped under military guard from the most famine-stricken parts of Ireland[31]…

The question is: Were there real options for prohibiting the food exports? Or, if the problem was acknowledged, were there any significant efforts to help Finnish or Irish people? As there were attempts to help the victims of famine, both the governments in London and Helsinki were unable and unwilling to act in the situation. As the opinions of politicians were divided, help efforts were slow and hazardous. Prevailing attitudes of the era certainly affected this. In Finland, famous writer Zacharias Topelius wrote as follows:

Here nature is a strict mother. It does not cherish its children with idleness and abundance. It demands of them hard work, much patience and self-denial. If they do not want to work and suffer, **they must starve and die**. But as a reward comes a steely and a healthy body, a brave and an enduring mind.[32]

While typical attitudes of the era were also clearly present in Britain, *The Economist* magazine of January 1847 wrote:

The people, rapidly increasing, have been reduced, by acts for which **they are chiefly to blame**, to a sole reliance on the precarious crop of potatoes.[33]

A typical interpretation of history would summarize the causes of Irish and Finnish famines as a combination of natural factors, social and production structures, combined with the attitudes of the upper classes and the laissez-faire economics practiced in both countries. Unfortunately, extreme historical events have long reverberations that affect up to four generations, sometimes even longer. According to Forsberg, the length of the cycle of historical interpretation is about four generations, i.e., a period of 100 years. Fifty years after the events, people who remember the event and people who build their own interpretation of the same events coexist at the same time.[34] In the end, the experiences of the previous generations dissolve in the fourth generation and thus the world gradually changes and renews itself.

From the perspective of mnemohistory, the mental memory in Finland of the famine affected the civil war of 1917, in which the external causes were division of the nation into socialists, known as the reds, and the legal senates parties, known as the whites. During the civil war Germany supported the whites, while the reds were supported by the newborn Soviet Union. According to Forsberg, the 50-year difference between 1867 and 1918 in Finland reflected the interpretation of reality in the background of the civil war.[35] The mental and emotional ballast created by the events of the famine received a new interpretation, which justified the rebellion by appealing to social inequality. A mnemohistory perspective suggests that the rise of socialism must have been at least partially guided by the fear of a recurrence of famine, even if no one was necessarily aware of this reason.

In Ireland, the interpretation of the past has always been at the heart of national conflicts, whether due to external causes such as the conditions of the peasantry, conflicts between Protestants and Roman Catholicism, or ancestral hatred of outside observers. According to Ian McBride, Irish history is almost non-existent because the problems of the past are being relived as current events. Resurgence of old fears and conflicts can only be explained by "some mystical form of transmission from generation to generation". In Ireland, current conflicts are expressed and connected to the past exceptionally strongly, for example, through various memorial rituals. A mnemohistory perspective argues that over time these commemorative events have become their own historical forces. An obvious example is the 1898 anniversary of the United Ireland Rebellion, which is not only an icon of resistance to British rule, but a symbol of the radicalization of Irish nationalism.[36] This story has served as a recurring justification or rationalization for feelings of fear and anger among the Irish. The past haunts the present moment and remodels itself in it.

A socionomic perspective, however, provides different accounts of why tragic societal events unfold and of how those events are recalled in subsequent eras. Socionomic theory proposes that the embrace of authoritarian politics and repressive, negative attitudes to fellow human beings is impelled by negative social mood, which leads eventually to tragic outcomes. In Hall's (2014) socionomic study of Ireland in the 1800s, he points out that the Irish Potato Famine began in the final years of a 128-year trend toward negative social mood.[37] It was one of a series of authoritarian tragedies that the English instigated or exacerbated during this period, as "English society attempted numerous ineffective schemes to fix economic problems and deal with an expanding underclass. These efforts included draconian trade restrictions that worsened the plight of the impoverished Irish over 13 decades".[38]

As so often in history, it is relatively easy to see and judge failures of the past. Yet, as social mood is endogenous and pre-conscious, it is often left unnoticed in real time. As such, it is difficult for society to see the prevalent prejudices of its own time. Indeed, society typically invents rationalizations to justify such prejudices in the heat of a negative mood trend.

In their article *Mood implications on social behaviour in complex societies: a literature review*, Italian researchers Alengoz, Castellani and Squazzoni (2017) restate one of Prechter's key socionomic points: Social mood shapes society's expectations for the future and experience of the present, especially in contexts of uncertainty. When negative social mood dominates, fear increases and the aggregate tenor and character of social events are likely to be weighted toward the negative.

From a socionomic perspective, shifts in social mood present shifts in societal preferences, perceptions and actions. Those shifts result not only in changes in the overall tenor and character of events but also in what parts of its own history (and the histories of others) a society emphasizes in contemporary discourse. As socionomics puts it, history follows the change of waves. When social mood is intensely negative, society calls to mind past grievances – or emphasizes new ones – to justify feelings of anger and discord. When social mood is intensely positive, society apologizes for past wrongs, lets bygones be bygones and seeks reconciliation and inclusion. These moments of reconciliation can be short-lived. When social mood turns deeply negative again, animosity between groups and the narratives that rationalize such feelings can be quickly resurfaced. And even if we are unaware of these aspects of history, we unconsciously experience something like what our predecessors *felt* at similar junctures in the social mood trend and thus behave in ways that have a similar tenor and character when those junctures recur, though our referents may differ. The tendency of history to repeat itself has thus a fundamental social dimension.

Notes

1 Kendall (1996/2018, 48).
2 In his research, Schmelzing (2020) *(Bank of England Staff Working Paper 845, 1–110)* refutes Piketty's (2014) assumptions about the unequalizing effect of human capital – he is, of course, not alone in his criticism.

3 Frost and Prechter (1978/2018, 159).
4 Huldén, Huldén and Heliövaara (2017, 77).
5 Lopez (1974).
6 Even before this, however, trading based on shares of agricultural products has been practiced in Bruges, Belgium as early as 1409 in front of the house of the *Van der Beurze* family. Similarly, international banking and related lending that started in Florence in 1252 foreshadowed the birth of a new economic system. The first speculative investment bubble was experienced as early as 1637, when in the Dutch "tulip mania" the value of investments fell by more than 95% from its peak (Ferguson, 2008).
7 In this speculative bubble, the subject of speculation was the shares of the South Sea Company. A similar collapse around the same time in France was the Mississippi Bubble.
8 Kendall (1996/2018, 205).
9 George Santayana the life of reason (1905–1906).
10 Frost and Prechter (1978/2018, 210).
11 Prechter (2002, 133).
12 Prechter (1992, 8–9).
13 Originally published in the September 2016 issue of *The Socionomist* under the title "Welcome to a Larger World with Fewer Friends: A Reversal in the 500-Year Trend Toward Globalization." Reprinted in Prechter (2017a, 377–390).
14 Hall, in Prechter (2017a, 377).
15 List quoted directly from Hall, in Prechter (2017a, 387).
16 Eysenck, H.J. (1956) The psychology of politics and the personality similarities between fascists and communists. *Psychological Bulletin, 53* (6). 431–438
17 Hall (2010a). Part of Hall's 2010 study is excerpted in Chapter 36 of Prechter (2017b).
18 Hall (2017).
19 Prechter (1999, 229–230).
20 Repucci (2020, 1–12).
21 Laland, Odling-Smee and Feldman (2000).
22 Bonn (2015).
23 If it is not really necessary, why would anyone with a relatively comfortable life question the status quo?
24 O'Flaherty (2015, 708).
25 Marek Tamm calls Mnemohistory as "the study of the afterlife of events".
26 Tamm (2013, 464).
27 Forsberg (2018, 494–495).
28 Jantunen and Ruosteenoja (2000).
29 Forsberg (2018, 496–497).
30 Professor Christine Kinealy in *History Ireland* magazine (1997, issue 5, pp. 32–36), as quoted by Ireland's Great Hunger Museum (n.d.). Exports in Famine Times. Retrieved from https://www.ighm.org/learn.html. The quote also appears in Hall's socionomic study of authoritarian events in Ireland: Hall (2014). Social mood can increase authoritarianism for decades: large-degree trends toward negative social mood impel tyrannical behavior. *The Socionomist*. March 2014, 7–12; reprinted under the title "Tyrannical Behavior Toward Ireland in the Mid-1800s" as Chapter 41 in Prechter (2017b).
31 Kinealy (1997, 32–33.)
32 Topelius (1875, 41).
33 Hall (2014/2017, 220).
34 Forsberg (2020, 76–77).
35 Forsberg (2020, 175).
36 McBride (2001, 2).

37 This negative mood trend began in 1720 and reached its negative extreme in 1848 as measured by British stock price data. The negative mood trend reached its extreme earlier, in 1784, in the Americas, as measured by U.S. stock price records (as shown in Figure 3.2).
38 Hall (2014). Social mood can increase authoritarianism for decades: large-degree trends toward negative social mood impel tyrannical behavior. *The Socionomist*. March 2014, 7–12; reprinted under the title "Tyrannical Behavior Toward Ireland in the Mid-1800s" as Chapter 41 in Prechter (2017b). Quote appears on p. 217 in Prechter (2017b).

References

Alengoz, L., Castellani, M. and Squazzoni, F. (2017) Mood implications on social behaviour in complex societies: a literature review. *Sociologica: Italian Journal of Sociology Online, 2017*(3), pp. 1–32.

Bonn G. (2015) Primary process emotion, identity, and culture: cultural identification's roots in basic motivation. *Frontiers in Psychology*, 6, 218. https://doi.org/10.3389/fpsyg.2015.00218

Ferguson, N. (2008) *The ascent of money: a financial history of the world*. London: Penguin Books.

Frost, A.J. and Prechter, R. (1978/2018) *Elliott wave principle—key to market behavior*. Gainesville, GA: New Classics Library.

Forsberg, H.M. (2020) *Famines in mnemohistory and national narratives in Finland and Ireland, c. 1850–1970* [PhD thesis]. Helsinki: University of Helsinki. http://urn.fi/URN:ISBN:978-951-51-3417-2

Forsberg, H.M. (2018) 'If they do not want to work and suffer, they must starve and die.' Irish and Finnish famine historiography compared. *Scandinavian Journal of History*, 43(4), pp. 484–514. https://doi.org/10.1080/03468755.2018.1466859

Hall, A. (2017) Social mood regulates perceptions of political normality. In: *Socionomic causality in politics: how social mood influences everything from elections to geopolitics*. Edited by Robert Prechter. Gainesville, GA: New Classics Library. pp. 185–190.

Hall, A. (2014/ 2017) Tyrannical behavior toward Ireland in the Mid-1800s. In: *Socionomic causality in politics: how social mood influences everything from elections to geopolitics*. Edited by Robert Prechter. Gainesville, GA: New Classics Library. pp. 217–223.

Hall, A. (2010b, May) Authoritarianism, Part II: the source of authoritarian expression and the road ahead. *The Socionomist*. pp. 1–6.

Hall, A. (2010a, April) Authoritarianism: the wave principle governs fear and the social desire to submit. *The Socionomist*. pp. 1–7.

Huldén, L., Huldén, L. and Heliövaara, K. (2017) *Rutto*. Helsinki: Like.

Jantunen, J. and Ruosteenoja, K. (2000) Weather conditions in Northern Europe in the exceptionally cold spring season of the famine year 1867. *Geophysica, 36*, pp. 69–84.

Kendall, P. (1996/2018) *Prechter's perspective*. Gainesville, GA: New Classics Library.

Kinealy, C. (1997) Food Exports from Ireland 1846-47. *History Ireland*, 5(1), 32–36. http://www.jstor.org/stable/27724428

Laland, K.N., Odling-Smee, J. and Feldman, M.W. (2000) Niche construction, biological evolution, and cultural change. *Behavioral and Brain Sciences, 23*, pp. 131–175. https://doi.org/10.1017/S0140525X00002417

Lopez, R.S. (1974) *The commercial revolution of the Middle Ages, 950–1350.* Cambridge: Cambridge University Press.

McBride, I. (2001) *History and memory in modern Ireland.* Cambridge: Cambridge University Press.

Nolan, D. (1971) Classifying and Analyzing Politico-Economic Systems. *The Individualist.* 1: 5–11.

O'Flaherty, E. (2015) Annales school. In: *International encyclopedia of the social & behavioral sciences.* Edited by James D. Wright. Oxford: Elsevier. pp. 708–713.

Piketty, T, (2014) *Capital in the twenty first century.* Belknap Press: An Imprint of Harvard University Press.

Prechter, R. (2022) *Last call.* Gainesville, GA: New Classic Library.

Prechter, R. (ed.). (2017b) *Socionomic causality in politics: how social mood influences everything from elections to geopolitics.* Gainesville, GA: Socionomics Institute Press.

Prechter, R. (ed.). (2017a) *Socionomic studies of society and culture: how social mood shapes trends from film to fashion.* Gainesville, GA: Socionomics Institute Press.

Prechter, R. (2002) *Conquer the crash: you can survive and prosper in a deflationary depression.* New York, NY: John Wiley & Sons.

Prechter, R. (1999) *The wave principle of human social behavior and the new science of socionomics.* Gainesville, GA: New Classics Library.

Prechter, R. (1992, September) Exclusionism: the next major trend. *The Elliott Wave Theorist.* pp. 8–10.

Repucci, S. (2020) *Freedom in the world 2020: a leaderless struggle for democracy.* Washington: Freedom House. https://freedomhouse.org/report/freedom-world/2020/leaderless-struggle-democracy

Schmelzing, Paul (2020). *Eight centuries of global real interest rates, R-G, and the 'suprasecular' decline, 1311–2018* (Staff working Paper No. 845). London: Bank of England. https://www.bankofengland.co.uk/-/media/boe/files/working-paper/2020/eight-centuries-of-global-real-interest-rates-r-g-and-thesuprasecular-decline-1311-2018

Tamm, M. (2013) Beyond history and memory: new perspectives in memory studies. *History Compass, 11*, pp. 458–473.

Topelius, Z. (1875) *Boken om vårt land.* Helsingfors: G.W. Eklunds förlag.

4

SOCIAL MOOD IN SOCIAL PHENOMENA

According to socionomic theory, waves of social mood appear in almost all matters related to human culture and phenomena in societies. In his 1985 report, "Popular Culture and the Stock Market" Robert Prechter presents a table of a wide range of trends that social mood regulates.[1]

Among the phenomena included are fashion colors, coverings and styles. As a positive mood trend waxes, ties become narrower and colors emerge and become brighter. At the positive mood extreme, bright colors dominate and short skirts allow you to show off your bare skin, a trend society embraces. As a negative mood trend waxes, drab colors become popular and ties widen. By the negative mood extreme, drab colors dominate, and long floor-length dresses or baggy trousers cover the body.

On college campuses, according to Prechter, university students work hard and have fun during a waxing positive mood trend. At the positive mood extreme, a "positive-minded save-the-world social concern" dominates campuses. He proposes that a waxing negative mood prompts rebellious and angry social concern. At a negative mood extreme, the atmosphere goes from student riots to profound silence.

Prechter's table also addresses trends in pop philosophy. During a waxing positive social mood trend, achievement is deemed possible and desirable. At the positive social mood extreme, a "love will save the world" attitude dominates. As social mood waxes negative, achievement is seen as a waste of time. And at the negative mood extreme, society embraces the view that "hate and destruction will give the world what it deserves".

Regarding popular music, Prechter proposes that as social mood waxes positive, upbeat songs in major keys come to the fore as melody emerges as a key ingredient. Lyrically, Prechter says any non-negative theme can be

DOI: 10.4324/9781003387237-5

TABLE 4.1 Some cultural expressions of social mood trends (Prechter 1999, 232–233)

Area of culture	Rising transition	Peak positive mood	Falling transition	Peak negative mood
CAMPUS TRENDS	Work hard, have fun	Positive-minded save-the-world social concern	Rebellious, angry social concern	From riots to sudden quiet
CREATIVITY	Positive mood creativity	Positive mood creative trend fully realized	Negative mood creativity; lack of creativity	Negative mood creative trend fully realized; destruction
DANCE	Partners together, tempo speeds up, partners separate	Partners apart, fast tempo	Partners come back together; tempos slow down	Partners together
FAMILY LIFE	Babies popular, family orientation, marriage	Trend reaches extreme	Children a negative value, divorce, "single" life preferred	Trend reaches extreme
FASHION (color)	Colors emerge	Bright colors dominate	Drabness emerges	Drab colors dominate
FASHION (covering)	Men's ties narrow	Bodies exposed, short skirts, bikinis for women, tight pants for men.	Men's ties widen	Bodies covered; floor-length dresses, baggy pants
FASHION (style)	"Correctness" stressed	Flamboyant individuality for men and woman	Anti-fashion fashions	Conservative dress returns
FITNESS/HEATLH	Health lifestyle, physical fitness practiced, encouraged	Body admired. Body-building peaks. Smoking. "junk" foods taboo.	Fitness fanaticism wanes rapidly. Social concern replaces concern with self.	"Working out" is out of fashion.

(Continued)

TABLE 4.1 (Continued)

Area of culture	Rising transition	Peak positive mood	Falling transition	Peak negative mood
GOOD vs. EVIL	Bad guys vs. good guys (movies, pro wrestling). Heroes celebrated	Everybody's a good guy	There are no bad guys and no good guys. Heroes trashed	Everybody's a bad guy
JUDGEMENTS	Answers are black and white	There is good in all	Who's to judge?	There is evil in all
MOVIES/TV/ LITERATURE	"G" rated themes, adventure	Celebrate life; upbeat, entertaining themes	Social concern, symbolism, heaviness, anti-heroes	Horror, dead-end themes
NOSTALGIA	Nostalgia for black-and-white values	Focus on now	Nostalgia for mythical simpler times (back to the earth)	Focus on now
POETRY	Structured	Lyrical	Anarchic	Ugly
POLITICIANS (Perceptions of)	Strengths magnified, weaknesses overlooked, forgiven or denied	Politicians revered (Camelot, "Teflon")	Weaknesses magnified, strengths overlooked or denied	Politicians hated or deified
POLITICS	Relative stability	Desire to maintain status quo	Old styles fail	Radical parties and solutions
POP ART	Structured, traditional	Colorful, wild, "alive"	Anarchic – anything goes	Deliberately ugly, heavy, sedate
POP MUSIC (Arrangement)	Simplicity peaks, complexity returns		Complexity peaks, simplicity returns	
POP MUSIC (Image)	Dirty, happy	Clean, happy	Clean, angry	Dirty, angry

(*Continued*)

TABLE 4.1 (Continued)

Area of culture	Rising transition	Peak positive mood	Falling transition	Peak negative mood
POP MUSIC (Melody)	Melody emerges as a key ingredient	Lilting, complex, inventive melodies and harmony	Melody is eclipsed by various elements: rhythm, arrangement	Little melody or chord structure
POP MUSIC (Mood)	Upbeat, major keys	Upbeat, major and minor keys	Minor keys, downbeat, arty	Distorted sounds, atonality, dissonance
POP PHILOSOPHY	Achievement is possible and desirable	Love will save the world	Achievement is a waste of time	Hate and destruction will give the world what it deserves
RELIGION	Conservative religion but increasingly subdominant	Religious tolerance and inclusiveness	Religion is openly questioned and passionately reintroduced	Powerful fundamentalist religions and cults
SEXUAL IMAGES	"Masculine" men and "feminine" women	Heterosexual images peak	"Feminine" caring men; "masculine", liberated women	Focus on alternative sexual styles
SPORTS	Clean "good guy" sports		Rough "bad guy" sports	
STOCK MARKET (popular valuation of productive enterprise)	Rising	Topping	Falling or correcting	Bottoming
WAR	Old wars fought and concluded	Little conflict	More conflict; new wars begin	New wars begin or intensify

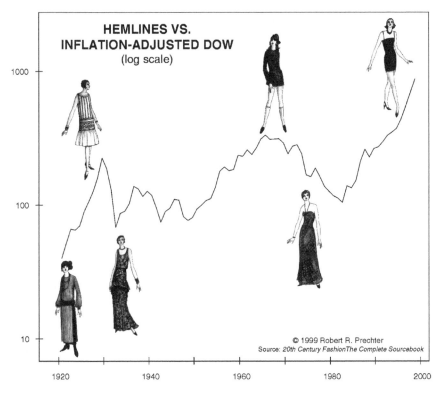

FIGURE 4.1   The skirt length indicator, 1920–1999 (Prechter 1999, 240).

socially acceptable at this point in the trend. At the positive mood extreme, lilting, complex and inventive melodies and harmonies are popular. Love songs and lyrics that express joyous celebration are common. As social mood waxes negative, minor keys, a downbeat mood and arty songs become more popular, while melody is de-emphasized in favor of rhythm, arrangement and other various elements. Lyrics reflect anxious, socially conscious themes. At the negative mood extreme, distorted sounds, atonality and dissonance find an audience, while there is little melody and chord structure. Songs of despair, violence and hate are more common.

In movies, television and literature, a waxing positive mood brings adventure and family-oriented "G-rated" themes. At the positive mood extreme, upbeat, entertaining themes that celebrate life are common. As social mood waxes negative, Prechter says social concern, anti-heroes, symbolism and heaviness are popular. At the negative mood extreme, society craves horror and dead-end themes.

In addition to the examples given in the table, numerous other areas of culture can serve as social mood indicators. For example, in cars, when mood waxes positive, both the power and size of the cars increase. Angular car designs are popular, while the favorite colors of cars, like in clothing fashion, are more varied and brighter. Silver can also become popular. When mood waxes negative, cars become smaller and rounded, and earthtone colors become common.[2]

To name but a handful more examples of cultural social mood indicators, consider the number of golf courses, the height records of skyscrapers, or, for example, the number of people attending cultural and sports events. The prevalence, extent and duration of these phenomena can be viewed as measures of social mood, just like more conventional financial and macroeconomic indicators. Examining these trends also provides an opportunity to identify where society is within the social mood trend and thereby predict and evaluate other cultural changes that are likely to occur.

Although it is easy to follow the logic behind the observations presented, their validation and data collection is, of course, another matter.

Cultural expressions, even though they may outwardly resemble each other, can still sometimes reflect different junctures within the social mood trend. For example, the great march on Washington led by Martin Luther King in 1963 with his famous speech *I have a dream* is not parallel to the *Black lives matter* protests of the 2020s, although on the surface seem to be related to the struggle of the Black community for equal rights. In this example, the Civil Rights Movement of the early-to-mid 1960s is associated with an inclusive positive mood, while the latter movement came to the fore during an exclusionary negative mood. However, when making such an interpretation, one must, of course, remember that in the 1960s the more militant Black Panther Party also had an impact on society. The rise of the Black Panther Party reflected the profound shift from positive to negative social mood that occurred in the mid-1960s. The Black Panther Party was founded in 1966, the first year of what would become a 16-year negative social mood trend as measured by the PPI-adjusted Dow Jones Industrial Average. The party dissolved in 1982, the final year of the negative mood trend.

The difficulty in interpreting socionomic theory is the fact that many kinds of phenomena occur in every time. Also, what captures society's attention varies. As discussed in Chapter 1, analyzing the relative frequency and intensity of positive mood expressions relative to negative mood expressions can help a socionomist to determine if the aggregate tenor and character of cultural trends are weighted toward the positive or the negative. The task of cultural history is to illuminate and interpret different eras from well-founded perspectives.

Socionomics is politically agnostic. Sometimes the interpretations made by socionomists may disturb the political right, sometimes the left. My reading of the theory is that socionomics accords with Hume's guillotine principle in that it strives to describe things as they are and not take a stand on how they should be. Strictly speaking, of course, no social theory is value neutral, and the socionomic research trend is no exception in this regard. The criterion of truth combined with the theory's internal and external consistency should be considered. On this basis, the theory can either be accepted or rejected. However, from the point of socionomic research, popular phenomena and especially extreme phenomena can be particularly interesting subjects of research. These areas often also attract the expressions of passions, which, in turn, makes them especially relevant as signs of the extremity of social mood.

The future of university education

Belief in education and its correlation with economic growth is probably the most common rationalization used to justify the necessity of higher education in Western societies. Socionomic theory does not believe in a causal connection between these two independent things.[3] According to socionomic theory, the popularity of higher education, growth in financial market prices and an expanding economy each reflects the underlying social mood. The popularity of higher education can be measured concretely in the number of students and degrees, as well as in increasingly expensive university tuition fees. The popularity of education and investment in education rise when people believe in it.

Despite the belief in education, verifying the economic benefits of educational investment is difficult, according to studies dealing with the issue. In the early stages of social development, this connection may seem clearer – the creation of missing technology and infrastructure seems necessary for the functioning of society and subsequent economic activity. Yet even then, socionomics would contend that the creation of infrastructure is insufficient to produce subsequent economic growth, as a trend toward negative social mood would simply result in infrastructure falling into neglect and disuse. And besides at a later stage of development, any causal connection between education, infrastructure creation and subsequent economic growth becomes blurred even further and, according to more critical studies, eventually disappears completely.[4] If education had a wider economic significance, it could be assumed that its quality would matter more than its quantity.

In a 2011 report, socionomist Alan Hall forecasted an approaching major peak in higher education which would be followed by an unfolding crisis.[5] Among the evidence he presented was Figure 4.2, which shows an Elliott wave count of five waves up in U.S. college enrollments per capita. As discussed in Chapter 2, fives waves are followed by a correction to the opposite direction under the Elliott wave model. Hall also pointed to the then-record popularity of higher education, record prices, a flood of student debt (a sign of optimism for both the borrower and the lender), so-called grade inflation and the then-booming for-profit college education industry as signs of extremely optimistic psychology regarding higher education. Socionomics teaches that from extremes in one direction, trends in the opposite direction unfold. He therefore anticipated reversals in each of these trends.

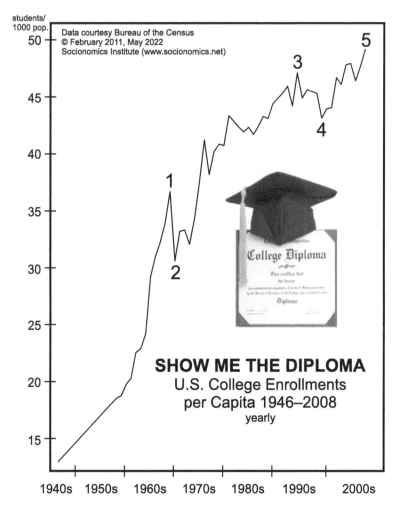

FIGURE 4.2   U.S. College Enrollments Per Capita, 1946–2008 (Hall 2011, 1).

The peaking process remains underway, but in the years since Hall's 2011 re-port, signs of a brewing crisis in higher education have become more apparent. Thompson (2022b) pointed out that the year of Hall's report marked a peak year for college enrollment, with enrollments falling a net 15% into 2019 (the latest year for which data were available at the time of Thompson's article).

Further signs of troubles in higher education include the number of people who have dropped out of university, the weakening of education funding, the lowering of degree requirements and especially general doubt about the value of higher education. The optimistic goal set by President Obama in his 2009 speech to Congress[6], according to which by 2020 60% of Americans aged 25–34 would have completed a university degree, has not been realized.[7]

While in his speech the president stated: "In a global economy, where the most valuable skill you can sell is your knowledge, a good education is no longer just a pathway to opportunity, it is a prerequisite", in reality the quantitative and qualitative goals of education have not been achieved. In fact, on the contrary, the situation has only become more difficult.[8]

Although socionomic studies on education focus mainly on the United States, I note that the problems and trends in higher education are very similar in all Western countries. At the same time as funding for universities tightens, social pressure to increase study places and the so-called quotas for special groups (affirmative action) cause more and more conflicts. The so-called cancel culture, where university personnel are afraid to bring up their thoughts and where some students actively try to report "wrong" teachers, is a reality in universities around the world,[9] and I believe reflects the falling transition of social mood of the era.

As students want high grades and complain more and more about the unfairness they experience, course grades have gradually experienced inflation. In my view, it is simpler for teachers to give a good grade than to demand a student's commitment to work. From the point of view of university teachers, this is also an occupational health and safety issue – from the point of view of university management, students are customers who should always be kept satisfied. If the student disputes his case, the teacher's position may be

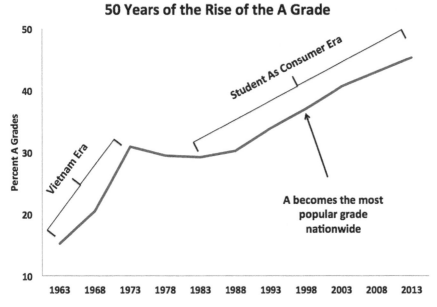

50 Years of the Rise of the A Grade

FIGURE 4.3   Increase in the share of A grades 1963–2013 (Stuart Rojstaczer: Grade inflation at American Colleges and Universities, https://www. gradeinflation.com/).

weak. However, the phenomenon that has become more and more obvious in recent years is already the result of a longer period of development, as the following figure shows:

Since 1998, the most common grade given in American universities has been A, i.e., the highest possible grade. I believe that without regulation or at least strong classification guidelines, grades in higher education institutions have less and less to do with the student's actual competence.[10]

In a development, I view as totally at odds with and living side-by-side with the feminist ideas and the puritanism of cancel culture, many female students have started financing their studies in risky ways - such as agreeing to potentially lucrative "romantic arrangements" with older men, known as sugar daddies.[11] Hall (2012) discussed the socionomic relevance of the phenomenon and mentioned *Seeking Arrangement*, which was founded in 2006, as one of the most popular service intermediaries in the field. In 2022, the company changed its name to seeking.com., while the number of its users has grown from 300,000 to 40 million members in 139 countries.

Internal corruption in universities and intensified competition have brought many other terms to the field, such as predatory publishers. These, often open access or open publication channels, accept articles for publication – usually for monetary compensation – without performing the promised quality checks, peer review, plagiarism check or ethical approval-like processes.[12] At the same time, mutual competition between researchers and the related mass publishing has increased considerably.[13] Mass publishing aims to promote either one's own interests and viewpoints (in which case the studies start to resemble more and more public addresses) or, on the other hand, simply to create the impression of success by adding one's own name to the study, even if one did not even participate in writing it.

Along with these phenomena, higher and higher university tuition fees have caused more and more people to doubt the sustainability of the entire higher education system. According to a recent report,[14] nearly a quarter of all university programs in the United States ($N = 10,000$) produce graduates, who do not earn enough to pay for their education within 20 years of graduation. This means that each year more than 350,000 students, or about 25% of students who have paid all of their education costs themselves (often with considerable debt), will not benefit financially from their degree at all. It's no wonder that student loan forgiveness programs and loan repayment relief are on the rise. While in 1997 the amount of student loans in the United States was 92 billion dollars, in 2020 the same figure is 1700 billion, or 1.7 trillion. Loan amounts have therefore increased by 1848% in 20 years. When the growth rate of loans is compared to other types of debt such as mortgages, vehicle finance, consumer credit or credit card debt (whose growth has also been worrying), no corresponding type of credit is comparable in terms of growth to student loans.

The growth of student loans has clearly exceeded most major economic indices and exceeded the amount of American credit card debt for the first time in 2010.[15] Student loans are completely comparable to the IT bubble of the 1990s or the housing loan bubble that preceded the financial crisis of 2008. However, from a human perspective, the issue is of course even bigger: it is worth asking what happens when entire age groups find that they have been "deceived" and become prisoners of their excessive loans without a realistic way out of the situation. When the social mood takes a turn for the worse, its consequences are also reflected in mental health. Increasing despair can be seen in the clear increase in use of mental health services by university students in the 2010s.[16]

Tightening competition, weakening funding, and doubts about the meaningfulness of scientific research each reflect a brewing sea change in public attitudes toward education. Look for the activities of universities to be evaluated more sharply in the public eye. According to socionomic theory, negative social mood impels a greater mistrust of science. Thus, a shift toward negative mood would likely only hasten the public's drift toward a less supportive posture toward universities. Also consider that Harvard and many other top Ivy League universities depend on endowments, much of which are invested in the financial markets. Fluctuations in the stock market, therefore, have a direct impact on their funding and operations. Hall (2011, 9) pointed out that in 2007–2009, Harvard University's endowment saw a rapid reduction of 30%. A comparable or even larger downturn will likely mean a significant reduction in funding and activities for such universities. Some universities will probably be closed down. Perhaps at the same time – in the remaining universities – there will be a return to the original ideas of the university, such as autonomy, the pursuit and cultivation of knowledge as well as good manners. And, to quote Hall (2009, 8), "remember: When most people see no light at the end of the tunnel, that's the socionomic signal that we are almost through it".

Attitudes toward drugs

Wilson's (2009) long-term socionomic study shows that social mood has regulated societal attitudes toward recreational drugs. He used the history of alcohol prohibition in the U.S. as a template to understand and anticipate trends in the probation of marijuana. Alcohol prohibition went into effect in the U.S. in 1920 and persisted through the waxing positive mood trend known as the Roaring '20s. The law restricting the use of alcohol was repealed in the United States in December 1933 in the midst of the severe negative social mood of the Great Depression. Finland shares a similar history, as its alcohol prohibition law expired in the spring of 1932 during the Depression as well. Since those times alcohol has been legal at least in western countries, but in its place mild drugs have remained as a contentious legislative issue.

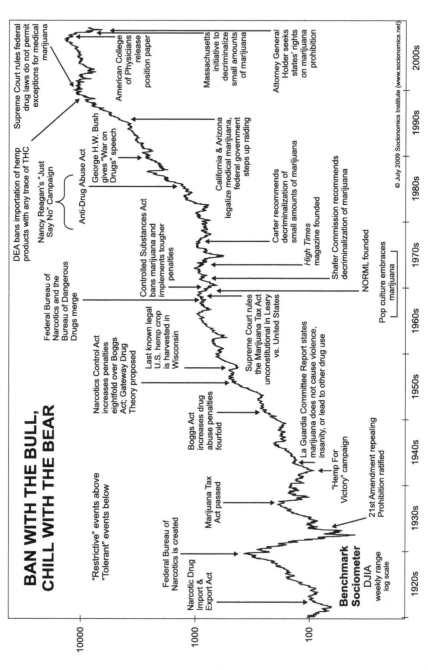

FIGURE 4.4   Drug legislation and the Dow Jones Industrial Average (Adapted from the version of Figure 1 from Wilson 2009 that was published in Prechter 2017b, p. 426).

Wilson's study was inspired by Prechter (1995), who made the socionomic connection between the modern War on Drugs and the earlier prohibition of alcohol and forecasted that marijuana prohibition would likewise be abandoned at the bottom of the next depression. Prechter (2003, 9) further forecasted that "The drug war will turn more violent. Eventually, possession and sale of recreational drugs will be decriminalized". Wilson, writing in 2009 amid the biggest financial market crisis since the Great Depression, sought to assess the likely trajectory for the prohibition of marijuana.

He found that changes in U.S. drug legislation have been associated with changes in social mood, as measured by the trends in the Dow Jones Industrial Average (DJIA). When mood waxes positive, society is less tolerant of recreational drugs and drug legislation is tightened. When mood waxes negative, society is more tolerant of recreational drugs and drug legislation is correspondingly loosened.

While the socially embraced values of the boom periods are clearly black and white "say no to drugs", when mood turns negative the moral attitudes become more ambiguous along the lines of "who's to judge?" Although attitudes toward drugs in the United States are sometimes also aligned along political lines, this kind of division does not reflect the attitudes of the entire population[17]. Since the social mood is stronger than different rationalized opinions, it also affects both parties, regardless of their traditional values.

As we now know, prohibition of recreational marijuana use began to be lifted in the U.S. after the financial crisis in 2012, when the state of Colorado legalized the recreational use of cannabis, and several other states followed suit. However, in the 2010s, another serious problem emerged alongside recreational drugs – the opioid crisis. While social mood was trending positively in 2017, as reflected by rising stock prices, Prechter (2017b, 441) observed that Attorney General Jeff Sessions sought to require federal prosecutors to seek the harshest sentences available for drug offenders. He forecasted that the extent and duration of the positive social mood would influence whether or not the legal system would follow through on Sessions' ambitions. Consistent with this forecast, we now know that the trend of social mood as reflected in share prices subsequently became more volatile, and Sessions' goals were not realized.

In this matter as well as in other matters, socionomics does not take a position on the morality of individual phenomena. However, socionomically informed investors, legislators and activists can use the trend of social mood to identify windows of opportunity where public opinion is favorable to their positions and act accordingly, if they so choose.

James Bond film ratings

In their studies of social mood and James Bond films, socionomic researchers Mark Galasiewski (2007) and Chuck Thompson (2012, 2016 and 2022a) reviewed the Internet Movie Database (IMDb) ratings given to Bond productions.[18] Collectively, the studies by Galasiewski and Thompson span from the 1962 *Dr. No* to the 2015 *Spectre*. IMDb is the largest movie database on the internet and contains movie plot descriptions, director and actor information, as well as movie scores that tens of thousands of people have given the movies on a scale of one to ten.

The researchers compared trends in the site's scores of Bond films to social mood as measured by the PPI-adjusted Dow Jones Industrial Average over the same period. The themes of the Bond films rely on clear dichotomies: In Bond's world, men are men and women are women; bad are bad and good are good, these criteria combined with fast cars, boyish humor and imaginative technical gimmicks make the films more likely to resonate in when social mood is positive.

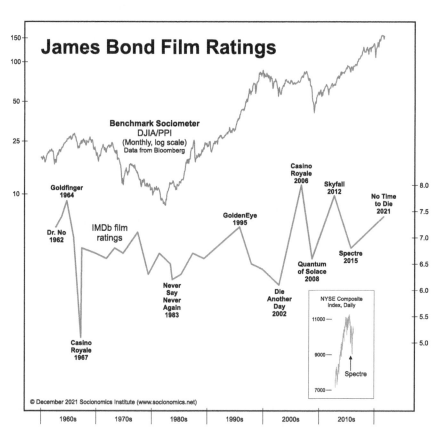

FIGURE 4.5   James Bond film ratings (Thompson 2022a, 11, with the inset added from the version of the chart shown in Prechter 2017a, 124. A version of the chart first appeared in Galasiewski (2007) and was updated by Thompson in subsequent publications with the release of additional Bond films).

Created by Ian Fleming, the spy and hero character appeared in book form for the first time in 1952. Although James Bond first appeared on television in 1954 in the program *Casino Royal* (starring Barry Nelson), the actual film debut was only in 1962. The film series has long been popular, even though the main character the performer has changed many times. Before the last film, there were already 25 Bond films. However, according to Galasiewski and Thompson's research, the public's appraisal of the films' quality has varied with trends in social mood.

The third film in the series *Goldfinger* (1964) marked an initial peak in Bond ratings, released as social mood was approaching a positive extreme. The subsequent 16-year-long negative mood trend corresponded with a trend toward lower ratings for the films, culminating with the lowly rated *Never Say Never Again*, released the year after the negative mood trend's extreme in 1983.

As mood then waxed positive in the 1980s and 1990s, the public's appraisal of Bond movies improved 1995s *GoldenEye* and especially 2006s *Casino Royale*, released the year before the stock market peak that preceded the Global Financial Crisis, have received high scores from viewers.

In more recent years, James Bond's masculinity has been questioned in accordance with the spirit of the time, as transitional phases in the social mood trend often see a blurring of socially recognized gender lines – and similarly, even the introduction of a female Bond to the series has been proposed. In terms of content, the Bonds of the 21st century are certainly more violent and darker than, for example, Roger Moore's lighter and more humorous Bond films from the 1980s.

Quantum of Solace's release coincided with the financial crisis in 2008 and was met with the lowest IMDb rating since 2002s *Die Another Day*, which was released the year of the Dow Jones Industrial Average's low in the dot-com bust. Audience ratings for 2012s *Skyfall* improved along with the social mood trend. Regarding the muted ratings for *Spectre* in 2015, Thompson (2016) pointed out that its release came during sharp decline in a broader sociometer, the New York Stock Exchange Composite Index, as shown in Figure 4.5.

Thompson (2016) also expressed that the perpetuation of the popularity of the more than 50-year-old series would likely hinge on the persistence of optimism in the social mood trend. At that time, the name of the upcoming Bond film was not yet known – much less its plot. Now everyone who has seen the film knows that *No Time to Die* seems to mark the end of an era. While James Bond hardly rises from the dead, it wouldn't be surprising to see the film series reinvented and brought back to life if lingering positive social mood persists or intensifies.

On habitus, slang and children's names

Generally, based on the words, expressions and dialect used by a person, conclusions can be made about their profession, social status or place of residence. The musical My Fair Lady (1954) tells the story of the English Eliza, who has the face of an angel, but the behavior and language of a street boy. Linguist Henry Higgins makes a bet with his friend whether he can train Eliza into a salon-worthy beauty in six months. Sworn bachelor Professor Higgins falls in love with his student, and, of course, the story has a happy ending. Like Henry Higgins, most of us are capable of similar intuitive conclusions when meeting a new person. Very quickly, based on the external essence, posture, face, and clothing, i.e., habitus of a person, we make assessments of their position in society. Language and speech reinforce our first impressions, which I believe are usually correct.

Socionomic research is very interested in cultural expressions that are related to many everyday things of people. As a legacy of many eras, words and sayings have become embedded in our language that reflect the mood of the respective era. Those who have lived in a certain time may remember where a saying originated, while others will probably never even think about it. In his study of popular slang, Hall (2016) proposed that popular sayings in positive-mood eras tend to be cheerful in nature (Wow, Right on, OMG),

FIGURE 4.6 Popular slang reflects social mood (Hall 2016, 4).

while popular sayings in negative-mood eras tend to take on more dark, sarcastic or even fatalistic features (shit happens; get a life; life's a bitch, and then you die).

The uniqueness of children's names in an era is similarly tied to social mood, according to research from Hall (2010). Hall cited findings from Twenge et al. (2010) that showed from 1880 to 2007, the share of individualistic

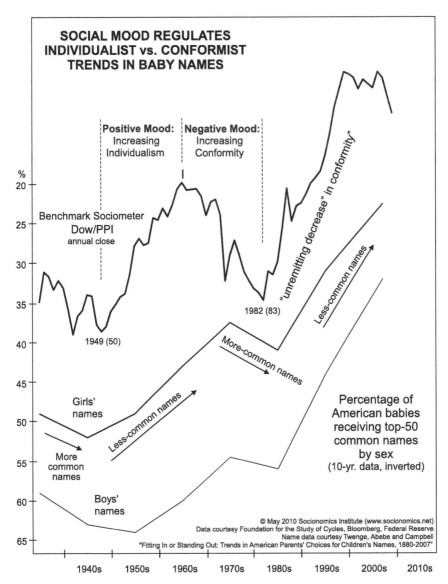

FIGURE 4.7 Social mood regulates individualist vs. conformist trends in baby names (Adapted from Hall 2010, 9).

names has increased, but the development had by no means been linear. Hall compared trends in social mood as measured by the PPI-adjusted Dow Jones Industrial Average to trends in Twenge et al.'s (2010) data on the annual share of children given one of the year's 50 most-common names. He found that as social mood waxed negative, parents expressed greater conformity in the names they chose for their children, while parents expressed more uniqueness and individuality in the names they chose for their children when mood waxed positive.

With highly elevated mood prevailing, very radical children's names have also become common. In 2020, Elon Musk named his child X Æ A-12, reminiscent of a car's license plate. In this matter, however, he just followed a trend where many other celebrities before him had given their children names such as Moxie CrimeFighter, Audio Science, Buddy Bear Maurice and River Rocket.[19] Already in 2016, the Swedish Parliament intervened in this growing trend by renewing the name law (Lag om personnamn 2016:1013), so that naming children, e.g., IKEA, Metallica or Google would not be possible. In September 2021, the Helsinki Administrative Court ruled that Lucifer is suitable as a Finnish first name. However, ironically, the trend toward more individualized names is profoundly social, as the desire for individual vs. conformist naming appears to be regulated by social mood. When social mood turns more negative, socionomic research suggests that we should anticipate a greater embrace of more common names.

On riots in London

In addition to data from the stock market, social mood researchers also have employed other sociometers, including those constructed from extensive internet data. The emotional or substantive connection of words to various social phenomena can be studied by mining mass online data. Applying this technique, the prevalence of words on the internet can be linked to various social phenomena, such as social unrest or, for example, the prevalence of various health conditions. According to researchers from the University of Bristol,[20] negative language use on Twitter foreshadowed the 2011 riots in London. Their data was based on 484,033,446 Tweets between July 2009 and January 2012.[21] According to their analysis, the outbreak of rioting was linked to a negative mood, which was reflected in a rising frequency of fear- and hate-related words on Twitter in the months prior to the outbreak of unrest. In addition to the fluctuating frequency of the vocabulary, it is noteworthy to consider the timing of significant social events, such as the British government's large budget cuts in 2010 and the August 2011 riots. Both of these are timed at or shortly after the peak of a rising wave of feelings of fear and anger:

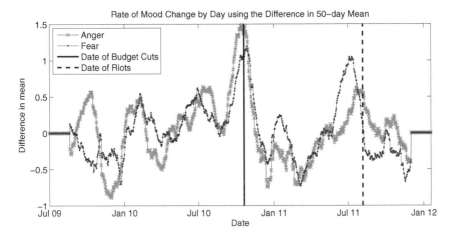

FIGURE 4.8   Anger and fear in London 2009–2012 measured from Twitter (Lansdall-Welfare; Lampos and Christianini, 2012).

According to socionomic research, major government actions that express social mood tend to occur after the mood trend has grown quite mature. One such manifestation that has grown salient in recent years is the outbreak of major wars.[22]

War and peace

From totalitarianism to appeasement, Gulag to glasnost, Russia's story consists of extremes.[23] The historical question of how to get along with Russia in practice fascinates researchers around the world. In Part V of its book *Socionomic Causality in Politics* (Prechter 2017b), the Socionomics Institute collects a series of its researchers' historical case studies and real-time analyses regarding Russia that were written and published from 2007–2016. The historical analyses cover more than 150 years of Russia's history, while the real-time analyses contain multiple forecasts that deserve to be introduced in detail.[24]

Hall (2007a and 2007b) presented a two-part historical socionomic study and real-time forecast for Russia's stock market and cultural manifestations. Hall used the Elliott wave model to identify five waves up in the Russian Trading System Index (RTSI), a primary stock index for the country. Recall from Chapter 2 that after the completion of five waves in one direction, the Elliott wave model calls for a correction to unfold in the opposite direction. He predicted a minimum drop of 62–75% in the RTSI, which would carry the index into the price territory of the previous fourth wave, a common retracement level.

FIGURE 4.9 RTSI's five ascending Elliott waves into 2007 (Hall 2007b, 3).

At the time, Russia was enjoying the height of a positive mood extreme economically, financially and geopolitically with respect to its image on the world stage. Russia appeared to be withdrawing its troops from Georgian Ossetia, where they had been since 1991. However, despite this positive news, Hall warned that a decline in the RTSI of the magnitude he foresaw would signal a sharp shift toward negative social mood, which would result in reversal of Russia's image on the world stage and its embrace of a more aggressive military posture. He noted, for example, that a strong negative mood trend in Russia would raise the probability for Russian military intervention against its neighbors, naming Kosovo, Azerbaijan, Ukraine, Lithuania, Poland, Georgia and Syria as possible targets.

In May 2008, six months after Hall's report, the RTSI registered a major high and then collapsed by 79.9% over the next eight months through the bottom of his target zone. As Hall also anticipated, the wave of negative social mood that created the reversal in the market also impelled a resurgence in the country's military posture. The month that the collapse in the market began, Russia sent its soldiers to the disputed region of Abkhazia. Tensions between the countries quickly escalated into a full-scale conflict between Georgia and Russia.[25]

Russia and its neighbors experienced a respite as a countertrend wave toward the positive unfolded from early 2009 to 2011 (Figure 4.11). This was a peaceful period between Russia and its neighboring countries. The war in Georgia was also short-lived. In April 2011, the downtrend resumed and another multi-year wave toward negative social mood unfolded. The plunge in the RTSI signaled a heightened probability for increased conflict, and on December 9, 2013, another researcher associate of the Socionomics Institute, Robert Folsom, warned about Russia's potential future actions, this time against Ukraine. He noted that not only was the RTSI in decline, but so was Ukraine's stock market, which had already fallen by some 75%. He forecasted that Ukraine's "neighbor to the east is particularly unlikely to tolerate much more instability before intervening".[26] Three months after this prediction, in March 2014, Russia occupied and annexed Crimea, ignoring international protests. Just earlier, Ukraine's pro-Russian president Yanukovych had been forced to relinquish power in the face of pressure from protesters. After these events, the crisis escalated in the eastern parts of Ukraine, in the regions of Luhansk and Donetsk, which declared themselves independent regions.

Despite these apt predictions, the Socionomics Institute does not claim to be able to tell what exactly will happen in the world or in the markets. Instead, it uses financial market indexes and other sociometers to assess the social mood trend and thereby anticipate the probable tenor and character of social expressions. The press, politicians or political commentators and historians, however, try to explain history with rationalizations. Such explanations can be, for example, "Russia seeks to increase its influence because it feels threatened by the West", "Ukraine plans to join NATO" or for example that "Russia had to protect its own population from fascist oppression in the Donbass region". Sometimes it's amazing how ridiculous reasons people and politicians come up with to justify their actions. However, it is worth understanding that the people making the claims really believe in their own thoughts and interpretations of the world. Unfortunately, the power and influence of social mood often goes unnoticed and, especially when social mood is intensely negative, it can lead to tragic results.

Going beyond the tenor and character of social events to make more specific forecasts is a challenge. In principle, for instance, Russia's negative mood could have motivated the country to seek conflict with a number of potential adversaries. As Folsom's forecast—and Hall's before it—demonstrate, an awareness of history and the political landscape in concert with the social mood trend can render it possible for a socionomist to at least weigh probabilities effectively. When mood turns negative, historical animosities can resurface and warm disputes in the present day can turn into hotter conflicts tomorrow. A negative mood creates and exacerbates crises, while a positive one brings with it attempts to solve them. The cause of wars is always found in the mood of society itself - not in geopolitics, even if someone claims otherwise.

Since the history of the modern Russian stock market exists only after the fall of the Soviet Union, Hall (2007a) used historical stock market data from the U.S. as a proxy for global social mood to contextualize major historical events in Russia over the course of nearly 150 years from a socionomic perspective. The result is Figure 4.10. The darkened time periods contain wars and crises.

A substantial drop in RTSI had preceded Russia's attacks on Georgia and Crimea, and during the writing of this book's original Finnish version, another drop in the RTSI prompted socionomists to anticipate the elevated likelihood that a third conflict would begin.[27]

One month after the original version of this book, *Laumavaiston varassa*, was published in Finland, Russia began its invasion of Ukraine, as the RTSI plunged. Researchers at Elliott Wave International and the Socionomics

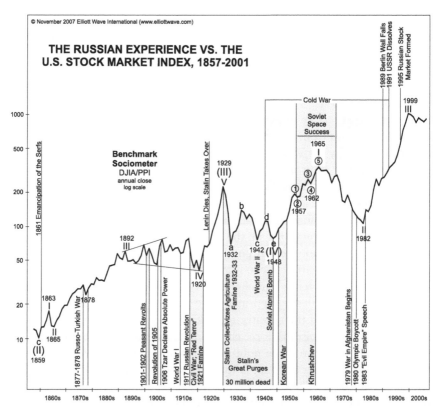

FIGURE 4.10   Waves of Russian history (Prechter 2017b, 278; adapted from the original version of a figure published in Hall 2007a, 3).

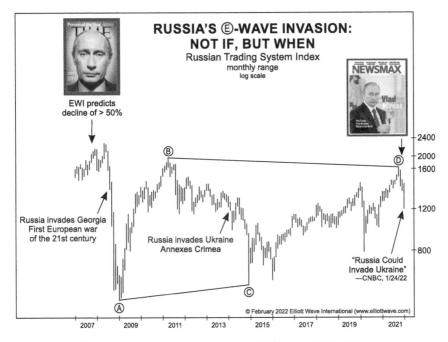

FIGURE 4.11   Three predictions that came true (Whitmer 2022, 38).

Institute anticipated this conflict as well, publishing Figure 4.11 three weeks before the invasion began.

In his book War and Peace, Leo Tolstoy reflects on the course of history:

What is the cause of historical events? Power. What is power? Power is the sum total of wills transferred to one person. On what condition are the wills of the masses transferred to one person? On condition that the person express the will of the whole people. That is, power is power. That is, power is a word the meaning of which we do not understand.

It would be interesting to hear what Tolstoy would say about the pattern above and Prechter's theory.

Notes

1 The table column headings are "rising transition," "peak positive mood," "falling transition," and "peak negative mood." Socionomists today, including Prechter, would eschew using directional language (e.g., "rising," "falling") and terms more germane to the stock market (e.g., "peak") to describe social mood and would instead use the phase labels similar to those reviewed in Chapter 1.

2 This analysis of car design trends summarizes the work of socionomist Mark Galasiewski, whose pair of 2006 studies on automobile styling are excerpted in Chapter 29 of Prechter (2017a).
3 According to a large-scale study that covered dataset on universities in nearly 1,500 regions in 78 countries since 1950 a 10% increase in the number of universities is associated with over 0.4% higher GDP per capita in a region. However, understanding the growth mechanisms through which the university effect works is not explained. In other words, the results of the study can be interpreted to support the socionomic hypotheses. (Valero and Reenen, 2019, 53–67).
4 Wolf (2002).
5 Hall (2011).
6 President Obama's 2020 College completion goal.
7 https://nces.ed.gov/programs/digest/d20/tables/dt20_104.60.asp
8 Kelderman (2020).
9 Norris (2021).
10 Rojstaczer and Healy (2012).
11 Mixon (2019).
12 Grudniewicz et al. (2019).
13 The aforementioned article published in Nature by Grudniewicz et al. (2019) has 35 authors, although the article is only two pages long. Although the article in question is of course a pamphlet, many other studies also seem to rely more on the number of researchers than on the actual content of the study.
14 Itzkowitz (2021).
15 Hall (2011, 2).
16 Sapadin and Hollander (2021).
17 Felson, Adamczyk and Thomas (2019).
18 These three studies are collected and excerpted as Chapter 10 in Prechter (2017a).
19 The socionomic significance of this trend is discussed in Hall (2017).
20 Lansdall-Welfare, Lampos and Christianini (2012).
21 For a different socionomic perspective on this study, see Chapter 32 of Prechter (2017b).
22 Prechter (1999, 259–260).
23 Hall (2007a, 2).
24 Prechter (2017b, 277–356).
25 Lampert, Hayden and Hall (2016).
26 Folsom (2013).
27 Chapter 2 introduced the basic three-wave corrective form and mentioned that more complex corrections are possible under the Elliott wave model. Russia's bear market since 2008 has been an example of the latter. For a full discussion of the various corrective forms that the Elliott wave model recognizes, see Frost and Prechter (1978/2018, 41–54).

References

Felson, J., Adamczyk, A. and Thomas, C. (2019) How and why have attitudes about cannabis legalization changed so much? *Social Science Research*, 78, pp. 12–27. https://doi.org/10.1016/j.ssresearch.2018.12.011

Folsom, R. (2013) Ukraine: the geographic center of a new cold war? Social Mood Watch. Socionomics.net.

Frost, A.J. and Prechter, R. (1978/2018). *Elliott wave principle—Key to market behavior*. Gainesville, GA: New Classics Library.

Galasiewski, M. (2007, April). A socionomic take on high-performance men, women and cars. *The Elliott Wave Theorist*. pp. 4–10.

Grudniewicz, A., Moher, D., Cobey, K.D., Bryson, G.L., Cukier, S., Allen, K., Ardern, C., Balcom, L., Barros, T., Berger, M., Buitrago C.J., Cugusi, L., Donaldson, M.R., Egger, M., Grahan, I.D., Hodgkinson, M., Khan, K.M., Mabizela, M., Manca, A. and Lalu, Manoj M. (2019) Predatory journals: no definition, no defence. *Nature,* 576, pp. 210–212. https://doi.org/10.1038/d41586-019-03759-y

Hall, A. (2017, December). Positive social mood continues to encourage unusual baby names. *The Socionomist.* pp. 1–5.

Hall, A. (2016) "Like, Ew! Grody to the Max!" Social mood influences the tenor of popular slang. *The Socionomist.* pp. 4–6. Republished under the title "'Like, Ew! Grody to the Max!' Social Mood Influences the Tone of Popular Slang" in: Prechter, R. (ed.). 2017a. *Socionomic studies of society and culture.* Gainesville, GA: Socionomics Institute Press. pp. 499–503.

Hall, A. (2012, March). The education industry is traversing a broad, multi-decade social mood peak. *The Socionomist.* pp. 1–6.

Hall, A. (2011, February) Back to the school of hard knocks? The education industry faces a multi-decade peak. *The Socionomist.* pp. 1–11. Republished in: Prechter, R. (ed.) 2017a. *Socionomic studies of society and culture.* Gainesville, GA: Socionomics Institute Press. pp. 359–375.

Hall, A. (2010, May). Socionomics can benefit sociology—case in point: baby names. *The Socionomist.* pp. 6–10. Republished in Prechter, R. (ed.). *Socionomic studies of society and culture.* Gainesville, GA: Socionomics Institute Press. pp. 491–498.

Hall, A. (2009, June). A socionomic view of epidemic disease, part II: stress, physiology, threats and strategies. *The Socionomist.* pp. 1–8.

Hall, A. (2007a) Sizing up a superpower: a socionomic study of Russia—Part I: Russian history and global social mood. *Global Market Perspective.* Special Report. Republished under the title "A Socionomic Study of Russa" in: Prechter, R. (ed.). 2017b. *Socionomic Causality in Politics.* Gainesville, GA: Socionomics Institute Press. pp. 277–292.

Hall, A. (2007b) Sizing up a superpower: a socionomic study of Russia—Part II: Social portents of extreme behavior in the resurging Russian Bear. *Global Market Perspective.* Special Report. Republished under the title "Sizing Up a Superpower: Portents of Extreme Behavior in the Next Russian Bear Market" in: Prechter, R. (ed.). 2017b. *Socionomic causality in politics.* Gainesville, GA: Socionomics Institute Press. pp. 293–306.

Itzkowitz, M. (2021) *Which college programs give students the best bang for their buck?* [Report] Washington, DC: Third Way. https://www.thirdway.org/report/which-college-programs-give-students-the-best-bang-for-their-buck

Kelderman, E. (2020, January) Happy New Year, higher ed: You've missed your completion goal. *The Chronical of Higher Education.* p. 7. https://www.chronicle.com/article/happy-new-year-higher-ed-youve-missed-your-completion-goal/

Lag om personnamn (2016:1013). lag-20161013-om-personnamn_sfs-2016-1013

Lampert, M., Hayden, A. and Hall, A. (2016). Behavioral finance beyond the markets: A real-time case study of Russia's military resurgence. *Journal of Behavioral Finance and Economics,* 5(1–2), pp. 145–164. Republished in: Prechter, R. (2017b). *Socionomic causality in politics.* Gainesville, GA: Socionomics Institute Press. pp. 337–356.

Lansdall-Welfare, T., Lampos, V. and Christianini, N. (2012) Effects of the recession on public mood in the UK. *Proceedings of the 21st International Conference on World Wide Web.* pp. 1221–1226. https://doi.org/10.1145/2187980.2188264

Mixon, F.G. (2019) Sugar daddy u: human capital investment and the university-based supply of 'romantic arrangements'. *Applied Economics, 51*(9), pp. 956–971. https://doi.org/10.1080/00036846.2018.1524129

Norris, P. (2021) Cancel culture: myth or reality? *Political Studies*, pp. 1–30. https://doi.org/10.1177/00323217211037023

Prechter, R. (2017b) *Socionomic causality in politics*. Gainesville, GA: Socionomics Institute Press.

Prechter, R. (2017a) *Socionomic studies of society and culture*. Gainesville, GA: Socionomics Institute Press.

Prechter, R. (2003, October). Some socionomic observations and forecasts. *The Elliott Wave Theorist*. pp. 5–10.

Prechter, R. (2003/2017). *Pioneering studies in socionomics*. Gainesville, GA: New Classics Library.

Prechter, R. (1999). *The wave principle of human social behavior and the new science of socionomics*. Gainesville, GA: New Classics Library.

Prechter, R. (1995, March). Cultural roundup. *The Elliott Wave Theorist*. p. 9.

Prechter, R. (1985, August). Popular culture and the stock market. *The Elliott Wave Theorist*. Special Report.

Rojstaczer, S. and Healy, C. (2012) Where A is ordinary: the evolution of American college and university grading, 1940-2009. *Teachers College Record, 114*(7), pp. 1–23. https://rampages.us/profjhonn/wp-content/uploads/sites/111/2015/10/Where-A-Is-Ordinary-2012.pdf

Sapadin, K. and Hollander, B.L.G. (2021) Distinguishing the need for crisis mental health services among college students. *Psychological Services, 19*(2), pp. 317–326. https://doi.org/10.1037/ser0000526

Thompson, C. (2022a, January) Mood riffs. *The Socionomist*. pp. 10–13.

Thompson, C. (2022b, June) Social mood continues to shape the fortunes of American higher education. *The Socionomist*. pp. 3–10.

Thompson, C. (2016, June). For James Bond, success is a matter of mood. *The Socionomist*. pp. 3–4.

Thompson, C. (2012, October). Film, fur and fright—a mixed bag for a mixed mood. *The Socionomist*. pp. 7–10.

Twenge, J.M., Abebe, E.M., and Campbell, W.K. (2010) Fitting in or standing out: trends in American parents' choices for children's names, 1880–2007. *Social Psychological and Personality Science, 1*(1), pp. 19–25. https://doi.org/10.1177/1948550609349515

Valero, A. and Reenen, J.V. (2019) The economic impact of universities: evidence from across the globe. *Economics of Education Review, 68*, pp. 53–67.

Whitmer, B. (2022, February). A deeper socionomic dive into Russia. *Global Market Perspective*. pp. 37–39.

Wilson, E. (2009, July) The coming collapse of a modern prohibition. *The Socionomist*. pp. 1–6. Republished under the title "The coming collapse of modern prohibition." In: Prechter, R. (ed.). (2017b) *Socionomic causality in politics*. Gainesville, GA: Socionomics Institute Press. pp. 425–433.

Wolf, A. (2002) *Does education matter? Myths about the education and economic growth*. London: Penguin books.

5

MIND, MEDIA AND SOCIAL CONCERNS

The social mood is reflected in world events, news and the whole atmosphere of society. Concretely, it affects how we spend our time, what we believe in and what we pay attention to. Contrary to what is conventionally thought, the media is not a neutral and objective transmitter of information, but as Marshall McLuhan[1] stated in his famous phrase: "the medium is the message". This means that the mode of operation of the media is primary in relation to the content it conveys. The contents are secondary in this respect. In the age of the Internet, I believe this has become increasingly clear. As the name suggests, the media, i.e., the mediator, adapts to the mood of the times and, with the advent of the Internet, amplifies.

In 1969, the physician and neuroscientist Paul Donald MacLean (1913–2007) presented the theory that the human brain consists of three separate brains.[2] In the 1990s, Robert Prechter noted the relevance of MacLean's triune brain ideas to socionomics. According to triune brain theory, the most primitive and oldest part of the human brain, the basal ganglia, or reptilian brain, regulates functions that are often called instinctive. These activities include the pursuit of safety, fear, desires, pleasure seeking and the "fight or flight" response. The second brain, or the limbic system, is inherited from lower mammals. Activities related to it include processes related to motivation and emotions, such as choosing a spouse, taking care of offspring, adapting to the social hierarchy, and choosing leaders. These two parts of the brain are more closely connected than the third and newest brain, the neocortex, which represents reason and judgment and creates rationalizations.

DOI: 10.4324/9781003387237-6

The Triune Brain
One mind, three brains

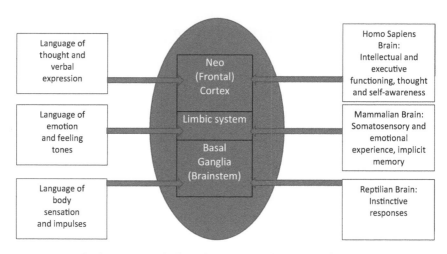

Language of thought and verbal expression

Neo (Frontal) Cortex

Homo Sapiens Brain: Intellectual and executive functioning, thought and self-awareness

Language of emotion and feeling tones

Limbic system

Mammalian Brain: Somatosensory and emotional experience, implicit memory

Basal Ganglia (Brainstem)

Language of body sensation and impulses

Reptilian Brain: Instinctive responses

FIGURE 5.1   The human mind, three brains according to Paul MacLean.[3]

Physiologically, the neocortex is powerless to control the impulses of the lower brain. Certain emotional reactions happen even before the neocortex has even had time to register the cause of the reaction – so the feeling arises before thinking. The part of the limbic system called the amygdala is only one synapse away from the thalamus (the part of the brain that regulates the body's reactions), while the hippocampus (the part of the brain associated with memory) is much further away.[4] In practice, this means that understanding things rationally is almost impossible for a person whose emotional state is not stable. It is also much easier to influence a person through emotions than by appealing to their reason. As already said, in contexts of uncertainty or arbitrariness, people think with their feelings.

This "thinking" proceeds as follows: Since the central purpose of the limbic system is related to the human instinct for self-preservation, it is able to attach to the impulses sent by the "lizard" (reptilian) brain very convincing emotional signals that end up in the neocortex with a delay. The stronger the signal, the more reliably the limbic system interprets it. In this situation, the system also uses the neocortex for support, which creates an *ex post* rationalization to justify the feelings.

The operating principles of the limbic system do not include consideration or temporal reflection, so its reactions and demands are immediate. Since the limbic system is also necessary for a person's personality and identity, people steadfastly defend the limbic system's demands and resist challenges to them.[5] This is why the saying "things argue, people don't" is so rarely true. The properties of the limbic system are therefore:

1 Speed – the limbic system is faster than the neocortex.
2 Scope – it regulates the amplitude of emotions, allowing powerful emotions to drown out other signals, such as those from the neocortex
3 Striving for immediate satisfaction – disassociated from time, the limbic system wants what it wants *now*.
4 Connecting feelings to identity – challenges to the limbic systems desires are perceived as challenges to a person's identity and are therefore powerfully resisted.[6]

When these basic processes are realized in a large group of people, the herd instinct comes into play. Its hallmarks are the desire to belong to the group, to be accepted as part of the group, and the associated conformism, i.e., avoidance of responsibility. Being in a herd, a person feels safe: 'Surely such a large crowd can't be wrong?' The opposite is also true: deviating from the crowd feels dangerous and risky.

Incidentally, I see these operating principles of the limbic system on display daily in modern news. Speed, constant exaggeration of things, sensationalism and capitalizing on heightened emotions are its typical features. Faster reporting and the desire to appease the public's emotional impulses have led to superficial journalism. At the same time, the modern nature of information transmission is such that news outlets reflect the mood of their audience. It is quite clear to me that this phenomenon is caused by and directly reflects the herding instinct.

To be able to form independent thinking, I believe the best way to do this is to consciously limit following the constantly offered news stream. Unfortunately, listening to one's own thoughts has to be given the space it deserves these days.

According to Prechter, sociometers vary with respect to how immediately they express social mood. Social actions that most immediately reflect social mood, according to Prechter, include stock market indexes, facial expressions and social media expressions. Social actions that express social mood with an intermediate delay include fashion, entertainment trends, product styling and depictions of heroes in pop culture. The intermediate delay is due to the time needed to produce such cultural artifacts. Social actions that take the most time to reflect social mood, what Prechter calls "eventual manifestations" of the mood trend, include political action, economic performance and social harmony or conflicts.

Socionomic studies have typically employed primary stock indexes as benchmark sociometers, as the stock market is among the domains where changes in social mood are most immediately registered. Evidence has emerged in recent years that suggests expressions on social media may register changes

THE RELATIVE TIMING OF SOCIONOMIC ACTIONS
PROVIDES A BASIS FOR SOCIAL PREDICTION
Increasing Lag Time Produces
Decreasing Precision of Wave Expression

leading
sociometers
(stock market)

lagging
sociometers
(pop culture, macroeconomy,
political action)

= immediate manifestations of social mood (leading sociometers)

(facial expressions, social media expressions, stock market, etc.)

= intermediate delay

(entertainment trends, fashion, product styling, hero depiction, etc.)

= eventual manifestations of social mood (lagging sociometers, or "news")

(economic performance, social harmony or conflict, political action, etc.)

FIGURE 5.2   Temporal variation of sociometers (Prechter 2016, 142).

in social mood even more swiftly than the stock market does.[7] Social media has been increasingly displacing traditional media, and the time lag between social mood changes and its expression online is apparently quite immediate.

When the World Wide Web was born in 1990, its structure was based on the principles of equality. These same principles also enabled its success as more and more people joined as its users and developers. Enthusiasm for the Internet and its positive possibilities reflected the positive social mood of the 1990s and resulted in the invention becoming integrated into our everyday life even to the extent that we take it for granted, like with electricity and water.[8] Today, nominal sociometers remain at or near all-time highs at a very large degree, as depicted in Figure 3.2 in Chapter 3, but on a nearer-term basis the past two decades have witnessed significant volatility. Western countries have undergone at least three financial crises: the dotcom bust of 2000–2002, the Global Financial Crisis in 2007–2009 and the market collapse in 2020. That turbulent mood has shown up not only in financial markets and economies but also in politics where polarization and rejections of centrism have become more common, and, to name a third example, in society's views of technology. The tech space has seen a tug-of-war between positive and negative mood influences, indicative of a mood trend in transition. On the one hand, online technology companies are among the most highly valued firms on earth. Yet on the other, views and discussions about the Internet have taken on fewer positive tones, and it is no longer seen universally as only a good thing. The disadvantages of the invention are increasingly emphasized in the cultural conversation and have manifested themselves in a way few anticipated or predicted back in the 1990s. Just as the free and open Internet was the culmination of a positive mood, a more volatile social mood has changed society's perception of and uses of the Internet in a commensurate direction.[9] In recent years, this has become more and more apparent.

Nowadays the major social media companies have begun to censor and isolate users from each other while governments (both totalitarian and democratic) monitor people's online behavior using the data they collect for their own purposes. The access to certain sites is restricted, the use of certain language of words can be censored and the users can be blocked from the services.

However, the freedom to use the Internet without someone spying, censoring, isolating or blocking is paralleled in history by the principles of documents like *the United States Constitution* of 1787 and Great Britain's 1215 *Great Book of Freedom, the Magna Carta.*[10] It is simply a matter of freedom and democracy. Unfortunately, in some countries this freedom has already been lost and state control has been taken to the extreme. Unfortunately, the impact of negative social mood is seen in expressions that are more and more dystopian in their nature.

Cyber threats are evolving and increasing at a fast pace as well. As an OECD report from 2012 explained:

> [Cyberthreats] are still initiated by criminal actors but also come from new sources, such as foreign states and political groups, and may have other motivations than money making, such as some types of "hacktivism" (Anonymous), destabilisation (Estonia in 2007), cyberespionage, sabotage (e.g., Stuxnet) and even military operations. Malicious actors are better organised, in particular to conceal their tracks, and the degree of sophistication has increased significantly, showing clear signs of professionalisation.[11]

Beyond the actions of governments and tech companies, consider that media consumers and social media users alike increasingly self-segregate by consuming content aligned to their political allegiances and joining social network echo chambers that reinforce ingroup identity and the vilification of outgroups. As a result, social interaction on the Internet is becoming more and more fragmented as users break up into separate "islands". It may be tempting to blame this societal polarization on the Internet itself, government policy, online algorithms or the profit motivations of tech and media companies. But consider that the very desire to break social consensus and cluster into smaller groups with more extreme views is a textbook manifestation of social mood as it transitions toward the negative, as illustrated in Figures 3.5–3.7 in Chapter 3. Increased cyber conflict along with more widespread surveillance and censorship of the Internet are also negative mood manifestations, each of which was expressly anticipated by socionomic research.[12]

In other words, all of these actors are simply dancing to the choreography that social mood demands. When mood grows more positive and optimistic, calls for more open expression on the Internet will find a wider audience, efforts from governments and media companies to censor will enjoy less political traction, and polarization will decrease in both online and offline settings.

Another sign of turbulence in the mood trend can be found in the tug-of-war between enthusiasm and horror in the public discourse over artificial intelligence. Thompson (2023) demonstrated that the tendency for society to express greater fear over innovations has recurred when mood has shifted toward the negative over at least the past 250 years.

Questions such as the following have become commonplace: Is AI an emergent self-regulating dynamic system? Does it imitate life or does it (already) possibly have its own conscious existence? What will happen if it gets the upper hand over humans, and if, like *Frankenstein*, it starts implementing its own built-in programs? And are people turning into machines themselves? What happens if a person loses their humanity in a world dominated by technology?

Far from being relegated to the far fringes of the social conversation, Microsoft's Bill Gates, Apple co-founder Steve Wozniak, PayPal and Tesla entrepreneur Elon Musk, and the late physicist Stephen Hawking have spoken publicly about the dangers of artificial intelligence to humanity. According to Wozniak, the supremacy of machines will reduce people to the level of pets. Elon Musk, on the other hand, warns humanity about the third world war, and Hawking claimed that artificial intelligence will replace humans when it starts to develop and reproduce itself in the future.

Beyond critiques of AI, critiques of social media and the Internet generally will likely follow the tide of social mood in their frequency and intensity. If mood becomes more negative, look for such critiques to become more frequent, intense and popular. It's already easy to find examples of such criticism. As Linus Torvalds bluntly stated: *I really hate social media – it's a disease.*[13]

In his book *The Internet Is Not the Answer*, Silicon Valley insider Andrew Keen (2015) critically analyzes the impact of the Internet on society. He says the list of problems brought by the Internet and social media is long:

1 The Internet concentrates power to monopolistic actors such as Amazon, Facebook and Google.
2 New Internet companies employ a minimal number of people.
3 Spying by companies and states has destroyed privacy.
4 Companies like Airbnb and Uber take advantage of their subcontractors.
5 Music, newspapers, photography and literature are in trouble for sharing free content.
6 Instead of democratic discussion, online rage and inferior behavior are increasing.
7 The Internet amplifies racism, sexism and bullying like a pandemic.
8 Loneliness and isolation increase, even though many present their lives on Instagram.
9 Virtually unmanned data centers collect information, and the companies own the data distributed to them for free.
10 Unlike states, large Internet companies do not have to bear responsibility for the social issues of society.

While Andrew Keen's book focuses more on what he perceives to be the external effects of the Internet on society, Jaron Lanier's (2018) *Ten Arguments to Delete Your Social Media Accounts Right Now* deals with what he argues is the direct impact of social media on human minds. Like Keen, Lanier has a Silicon Valley background. His ten arguments on social media are as follows:

1 **You are losing your free will**
    Algorithms type and bring you content that reinforces your prejudices, biases and preconceived notions about the world. By editing their news feeds and thus always returning to the same content, people themselves also reinforce this phenomenon.
2 **Quitting social media is the most finely targeted way to resist the insanity of our times**
    The psychological operating principle of social media follows the so-called BUMMER mechanics. The parts of this "machine" are[14]:

    a Attention acquisition leading to asshole supremacy. It can be seen, for example, in online discussions, where arguments usually turn very quickly into arguments, name-calling and even death threats.
    b Butting into everyone's lives. We are spied on and classified by our contacts and interests, based on our movement and other behavior. Here it's about so-called profiling. This information about us is merchandise, the buyers of which we know nothing about.

c Cramming content down people's throats. Based on profiling, we are fed things that are thought to be suitable for us. However, we are targeted by advertising that we cannot escape, even if we wanted to.

d Directing people's behaviors in the sneakiest way possible. In social media, people's emotional reactions are constantly tested as correlations to different news, ways of reading and content that are suitable for certain groups of readers.

e Earning money from letting the worst assholes secretly screw with everyone else. Social media platforms, for example, Facebook, are very rarely responsible for false communication or open pyramid schemes or other scams.

f Fake mobs and Faker society. For example, the so-called "tubers" with their millions of followers use bots to drive traffic to their sites. Fake publications, fake conferences and fake news are increasing every year. It follows that we no longer know what is true and what's even worse: who really cares anymore? According to Lanier, this all means fogging, i.e., the adaptation of an individual's beliefs to comply with outside interests.

3 **Social media is making you into an asshole**
Bad behavior, addictive Twitter rants and distortions – lying, cheating and swindling – are common to every citizen today, a fundamental right that politicians also diligently exercise.

4 **Social media is undermining truth**
Conspiracy theories, wild rumors and biased reporting effectively prevent us from seeing what is really true.

5 **Social media is making what you say meaningless**
In ancient Rome, the place for informal self-expression was the outer walls of the lavatory, where anyone could write whatever they wanted. Today this is called feedback systems or discussion boards. Both of these are written anonymously.

6 **Social media is destroying your capacity for empathy**
Putting yourself in the position of others is even more difficult, because people no longer meet anyone in real-life situations. It's easy to blame your bad feeling on "the others".

7 **Social media is making you unhappy**
Depression and mental health problems are increasing. Everyone else seems to be doing better than you. Nice vacation photos and beautiful selfies give a falsely beautiful image of the world, which may seem completely impossible to achieve.

8 **Social media doesn't want you to have economic dignity**
You can download everything for "free" – then you don't have to buy discs, books or read magazines. Many creative professions are withering and brick-and-mortar stores are dying. How did you think you would

earn a living if you are not active in the physical world?
 9 **Social media is making politics impossible**
    One-issue movements capture the contents of politics for themselves
    and use propaganda to shape public opinion.
10 **Social media hates your soul**
    You are not special, or you can be anything. Or maybe you're nothing?

Socionomically, the veracity of these claims or their lack thereof is secondary (at best) for assessing their probable popularity. Rather, what matters most is the alignment of their tenor and character with the social mood trend. Critiques similar in tone to those from Keen and Lanier will likely find a greater audience if negative social mood were to intensify.

It is also important to consider how social mood regulates the nature of expression on the Internet. Negative social mood encourages a greater frequency and extremity of discord, polarization, anger, anxiety and pessimism.[15] An undeniable fact is that these harmful effects on expression are visible on the Internet, and we can expect them to be even more so if social mood were to grow more negative.[16] Since Robert Prechter states[17] that social mood governs the tenor and character of social actions, there is no reason to assume that human expression on the Internet or social media are an exception in this regard. Whether it is a medium of mass communication – radio, television or the Internet – or the human being himself, humans are prone to the herd mentality and to express social mood.

As surprising as it may sound, according to socionomic theory, communication technology does not amplify social mood, because there is no feedback loop from technology back to social mood. If there was, then negative social mood would create more negative discourse, that discourse would be shared through communications technology, which would then create more negative mood, ad infinitum. Since mood trends fluctuate, such cannot be the case. Instead, when the mood changes, the tenor and character of the public discourse simply follow. Communication technology does, however, make it easier to view and share collective rationalizations, allowing rationalizations to spread faster than they could otherwise.

Epidemics and social mood

In world historical events, infectious disease epidemics have appeared as part of social upheavals. Socionomics proposes that the upheavals, such as financial crises, political crises and wars, and the epidemics themselves are symptoms of negative social mood. As Prechter (1994, 7) observed, "For whatever reason, disease sometimes plays a prominent role in major corrective periods". He further explained in a 2004 report that while conventionally it is thought that the onset of epidemics cause people to be fearful and depressed, the socionomic interpretation of the causality is that fearful and depressed are susceptible to the onset of epidemics.[18]

Consistent with this hypothesis, Hall (2009) presented evidence that suggests epidemics have a greater likelihood to erupt near negative mood extremes in the country of their origin, while the outbreak of disease can persist into the subsequent trend toward positive mood.[19] I note that sometimes epidemics have also marked the end of cultures or eras.

In 1519, a group of 600 Spanish soldiers led by Hernán Cortés landed in Mexico with the goal of conquering the Aztec Empire and their capital, Tenochtitlán. The Spanish's success in the war was based on their weapon technology, but the final victory was brought by smallpox, which, as a result of the 1520 epidemic, killed up to half of the region's population. The Spanish were not infected by the disease, as they were immune to it. It is estimated that by 1618, the original population of 20 million people in the region would have collapsed to 1.6 million.[20] Although our knowledge of the social mood of the Aztec Empire before the events is speculative, I propose that their religion (with human sacrifices) and the eschatology included in the religion give reason to assume that they foresaw their fate.[21]

In Europe, Justinian's plague killed a large part of the inhabitants of the city of Constantinople in 542, and later it is estimated to have killed even half of the entire population of the Byzantine Empire.[22] From the eastern Mediterranean region, the plague epidemic spread to different parts of Europe, North Africa and the Middle East. The events were preceded by a sudden cooling of the climate, probably due to a volcanic eruption in 536. According to contemporary sources, the sun shone for only four hours a day and the average temperature dropped about three degrees below normal.[23]

According to McNeill (1974), professor Chen's (1940) listing[24] of epidemics in China from 243 BCE to 1911 includes documentation of 291 known epidemics. Infectious diseases have therefore occurred in China every eight years, on average, during the 2,000 years.[25] In addition to the plague and smallpox, other infectious diseases that have affected humanity have included influenza, tuberculosis, spotted fever, syphilis and AIDS (32 million deaths).

In 1918–1919, the Spanish flu is estimated to have killed around 3–5% of the world's population. Depending on the source, the death toll varies from 17 million to 50 million or even 100 million people.[26] Figure 5.3, from Hall (2009, 4), shows that the Spanish flu epidemic was just one of a collection of crises that broke out toward the end of a more than two-decade-long negative mood trend at the beginning of the 20th century. Other such negative mood manifestations in the period included World War I, large outbreaks of polio, and the Encephalitis lethargica "sleeping sickness" epidemic. The underlying etiology of the latter has remained enigmatic to epidemiologists.[27]

Other epidemics of the 20th century include the 1957–1959 Asian flu, which epidemiologists estimate resulted in 1.1 million deaths, and the

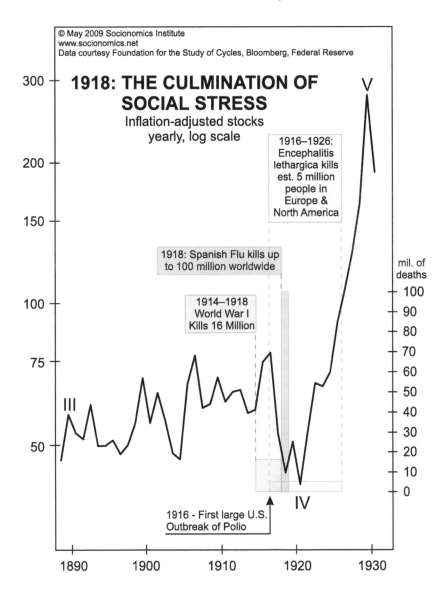

FIGURE 5.3 1918: The culmination of social stress (Hall 2009, 4).

1968–1969 Hong Kong flu, which resulted in between 1 and 4 million deaths.[28] Stock market data for China, the country where epidemiologists believe the 1957 Asian flu originated, are unavailable around the time of the outbreak. But Galasiewski (2008, 8) showed that the 1968 Hong Kong flu epidemic erupted in the wake of a three-year, 50% decline in Hong Kong's primary stock index, the Hang Seng.

The number of victims of the 2009 swine flu has been reported to be around 575,000 people.[29] Epidemiologists have traced the origins of the outbreak to Mexico, and socionomists note that it erupted near the nadir of the Global Financial Crisis, a negative extreme in social mood.[30]

Figure 5.4 shows the timing of the Covid-19 outbreak in the context of prior smaller-degree infectious disease outbreaks and the history of social mood in China, the outbreaks' country of origin. The Covid-19 pandemic erupted after more than a dozen years of a negative mood trend in China, as measured by the country's primary stock index, the Shanghai Composite.

A socionomic perspective can contextualize the timing of the origin of the outbreak, and it can also rebut the conventional narrative that global markets fell in 2020 due to the epidemic. Consider Figure 5.5, which shows the swiftest descent from an all-time in the history of the Dow Jones Industrial Average *preceded* the acceleration in Covid-19 cases in the United States.

FIGURE 5.4   Shanghai Composite Index and epidemics (Lampert and Galasiewski 2020, 8).

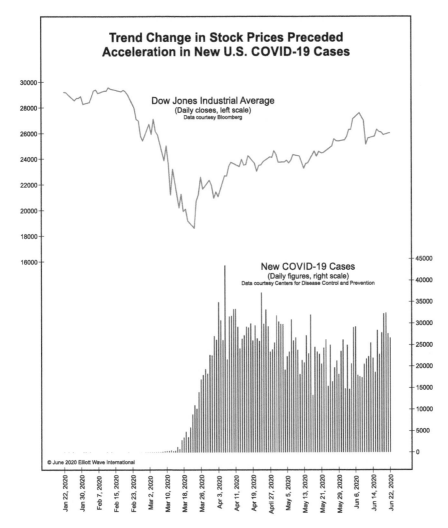

FIGURE 5.5   Trend change in stock prices preceded acceleration in new U.S. Covid-19 cases. Adapted from Lampert (2020).

The stock market then soared as the epidemic worsened and the largest quarterly contraction in GDP on record unfolded.[31] These events make little sense absent a socionomic perspective, which understands that social mood is psychologically endogenous and not prompted by outside forces like epidemics or economic growth. Rather, the severe negative mood trend that registered quickly in the stock market eventually prompted numerous other hallmark negative mood manifestations, such as a turn toward authoritarianism, an economic contraction, rising unemployment and societal unrest. (See Figure 5.2 for a depiction of the relative timing of socionomic actions.)

The persistently rising trend in the stock market from the late March 2020 low indicated that while the trend toward negative social mood was severe, it was likely to be relatively short-lived. And indeed, the most draconian of the authoritarian policies, the economic contraction, the spike in unemployment and the wave of societal unrest were also relatively short-lived, lasting on the order of months instead of, say, several years. The epidemic itself served as a referent that society used to rationalize its feelings and actions born of the deep insecurity, fear and anxiety that a severe wave of negative social mood impelled.

Two branches of transcendence – environmentalism and capitalism

The basic works of the environmental movement by Ralph Waldo Emerson (1803–1882) and Henry David Thoreau (1817–1862) represent transcendental philosophy. Its thinking includes a belief in the essential unity of all creation, the innate goodness of humanity and the importance of intuition. Combining the ideas of Goethe, Kant and Swedenborg with Eastern philosophy, Emerson presented his thinking for the first time in his book *Nature* (1836) and later in his numerous essays and presentations around the United States. Thoreau's works *Walden* or its other name *Life in the Woods* (1854) and *Civil Disobedience* (1849) contain the central action models and ideas of the current environmental movement.

Interestingly, the ideas of modern capitalism and those of American transcendentalism both represent a Calvinist belief, in which the former humankind is liberated through economic growth, and in the latter through nature.[32] In capitalism, economic growth and wealth are intrinsic values, which according to Max Weber's interpretation are the result of efficiency, responsibility for results, and determined pursuit of profit. Financial success, under this perspective, is thus a sign of God's favor.[33] Because man is separate from God, it is thought that nature and man are also separate from each other. Since in this view man is fundamentally evil (original sin), and his uninformed intuition leads him astray, rational analysis and decision-making are preferred means to achieve goals. Success and abundance are signs of true faith in Calvinism.

The central tenets of the environmental movement, however, include cutting out all unnecessary excess, the right kind of diet and refusal of meat products, eschatology, i.e., fears of the end of the world, and rituals such as recycling, Earth Day and opposition to motoring or furs. Natural products and medicines are preferred over "non-natural" products and medicines – limiting the number of children is also part of this credo. The movement prescribes a sort of religious asceticism as a way of life that others should also follow.[34] Man is fundamentally good and problems, in Rousseau fashion, are fundamentally the cause of a corrupt society. While the environmental movement and its romantic world of ideas emphasize collectivism, its counterpart capitalism is inherently individualistic in nature. I see both of these movements as essentially religious beliefs that are subordinated to the social mood, which can be seen in the alternation of the predominance of these faith trends over the decades.

For its part, the Socionomics Institute does not wade into the waters of waxing philosophical about the transcendent qualities of capitalism or environmentalism. Rather, its research on environmentalism is solely interested in contextualizing and anticipating the timing of the movement's periods of success and setbacks. Figure 5.6, adapted from Hall (2008), shows periods of advancement and decline in the environmental movement on a chart of the Thomson Reuters Equal Weight Continuous Commodity Index. Hall observed that the environmental movement's periods of advancement tended to coincide with periods of rising commodity prices, while the movement's periods of setback tended to coincide with periods of declining commodity prices.

From a socionomic point of view, Hall accounted for the relationship by proposing that, unlike rising stock prices, rising commodity prices are typically associated with feelings of fear, especially fear of resource shortages. The environmental movement's message thereby is more likely to resonate when the public is primed to fear running out of the planet's resources.

The small number of favorable events for the environmental movement in Figure 5.6 during the 1950s and 1980s–1990s is noteworthy, as those were periods of commodity price declines. Also note the prevalence of environmental disasters in those periods. The environmental movement was not winning, and neither was the environment.

Yet the figure shows that the 1960s–1970s and 2000s were times when the environmental movement thrived while commodity prices advanced. A classic of the environmental movement, *The Limits to Growth*, commissioned by the Club of Rome, was published during the first of these periods, in 1972. This book, which sold around 30 million copies, predicted that the exploitation and overconsumption of natural resources would inevitably lead to social, economic and environmental disasters after 2020. Some of the estimates in the original work, for example, regarding population growth, were correct; other estimates, such as for the growth of industrial production, were overestimated; while the analysis dealing with the sufficiency of raw materials was nowhere near correct.[35] An objective evaluation of the 1972 report is not easy due to the different scenarios it contains, and it was later updated in subsequent publications.

However, socionomics is not concerned with whether the information and forecasts in *The Limits to Growth* were right or wrong. Rather, socionomics seeks merely to account for the timing of the report's popularity. It does so

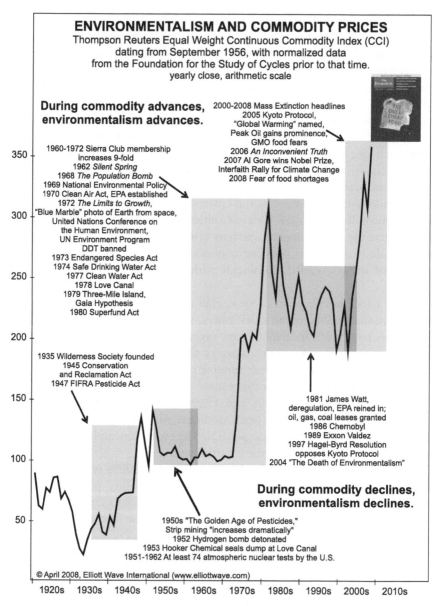

FIGURE 5.6 Environmentalism and commodity prices (Hall 2008, 11).

through the observation that its publication came in the context of waxing societal fears of environmental shortages, which was simultaneously reflected in a rising trend in commodity prices. When fears of shortages waned, commodity prices declined and the environmental movement faced a setback in the 1980s.

Notes

1 Understanding media: the extensions of man (1964).
2 Lambert (2003, 345).
3 Interaction Design Foundation, https://www.interaction-design.org/literature/article/the-concept-of-the-triune-brain
4 LeDoux (1989).
5 Prechter (1999, 150–151).
6 Prechter (1999, 151).
7 For further details, see Chapter 9 of Prechter (2016).
8 Berners-Lee (2010, 80).
9 Hall (2017).
10 Berners-Lee (2010, 82).
11 OECD (2012).
12 See Hall (2010a, 2010b).
13 Konttinen (2019). Torvalds is a Finnish-American software engineer who is the creator and, historically, the main developer of the Linux and Android systems.
14 Lanier (2018, 29).
15 For a fuller list of negative mood traits, see Table 1.1 in Chapter 1.
16 Ingibjorg et al. (2019).
17 Prechter (1999, 220).
18 Prechter (2004, 1).
19 Hall (2009, 1).
20 Diamond (1999, 210).
21 Read (1986).
22 Horgan (2014).
23 Huldén, Huldén and Heliövaara (2017, 57–64).
24 McNeill (1976, 260–269).
25 McNeill (1976, 260–269).
26 Spreeuwenberg, Kroneman and Paget (2018), Patterson and Pyle (1991, 14–15).
27 McCall et al. (2008).
28 Viboud et al. (2016).
29 Rogers (2020).
30 Lampert and Galasiewski (2020, 6).
31 Cullen (2020).
32 Nelson (2010).
33 According to the doctrine of predestination, which is part of Calvinism, man cannot influence his eternal destiny. According to Weber, this feature, which is stronger in Calvinism than in Lutheranism, has influenced the development of capitalism. Uncertainty about man's ultimate destiny is replaced by worldly success.
34 Nelson (2014, 266–271).
35 Lomborg (2012).

References

Berners-Lee, T. (2010) Long live the Web: a call for continued open standards and neutrality. *Scientific American, 303*(6), pp. 80–85. http://www.jstor.org/stable/26002308

Cullen, T. (2020) Second-quarter GDP plunged by worst-ever 31.7% as economy went into lockdown. *CNBC*. April 27. https://www.cnbc.com/2020/08/27/us-gdp-q2-2020-second-reading.html

Diamond, J. (1999) *Guns, germs, and steel: the fates of human societies.* New York, NY: W. W. Norton & Company.

Galasiewski, M. (2008) Cultural trends: infectious disease. *Global Market Perspective* (Special Report). April, pp. 7–9.

Hall, A. (2017) A socionomic view of the necessity of cyber conflict and the future of the Internet: the Internet is evolving an immune system. *The Elliott Wave Theorist*, May, pp. 2–10.

Hall, A. (2010b) Authoritarianism, Part II: the source of authoritarian expression, and the road ahead. *The Socionomist*, May, pp. 1–6.

Hall, A. (2010) Authoritarianism: the wave principle governs fear and the social desire to submit. *The Socionomist*, April, pp. 1–8.

Hall, A. (2009) A socionomic view of epidemic disease: a looming season of susceptibility. *The Socionomist*, May, pp. 1–6.

Hall, A. (2008) Elliott waves regulate commodity prices and expressions of environmentalism. *The Elliott Wave Theorist*, pp. 7–12. Republished under the title Elliott waves simultaneously regulate commodity prices and expression of environmentalism. In: *Socionomic studies of society and culture*. Edited by Robert Prechter. Gainesville, GA: Socionomics Institute Press. pp. 537–542.

Horgan, J. (2014) Justinian's plague (541–542 CE). *Ancient History Encyclopaedia*. December 26. https://www.worldhistory.org/article/782/justinians-plague-541-542-ce/

Huldén, L., Huldén, L. and Heliövaara K. (2017) *Rutto*. Helsinki: Like.

Ingibjorg, E.T., Rannveig, S., Bryndis, B.A., Allegrante, J.P. and Inga, D.S. (2019) Active and passive social media use and symptoms of anxiety and depressed mood among Icelandic adolescents. *Cyberpsychology, Behavior and Social Networking*, 22(8), pp. 535–542. https://doi.org/10.1089/cyber.2019.0079

Keen, A. (2015) *The Internet is not the answer*. London: Atlantic Books.

Konttinen, E. (2019) *Linus Torvalds: "Minä todella inhoan sosiaalista mediaa – se on sairaus" Uusi Suomi (8.4.2019)*. https://www.uusisuomi.fi/uutiset/linustorvalds-mina-todella-inhoan-sosiaalista-mediaa-se-on-sairaus/719f72c7-45ea-3af7-8fdb-b265f-60d04b4

Lampert, M. and Galasiewski, M. (2020) Coronavirus: why china, why now, what's next? *The Socionomist*, March, pp. 3–8.

Lampert, M. (2020) Thrive in the age of turbulence: five game-changing social trends you can anticipate. Socionomics Institute. Webinar.

Lambert, K.G. (2003) The life and career of Paul MacLean: a journey toward neurobiological and social harmony. *Physiology & Behavior*, 79(3), pp. 343–349. https://doi.org/10.1016/s0031-9384(03)00147-1

Lanier, J. (2018) *Ten arguments for deleting your social media accounts right now*. New York, NY: Henry Holt and Company.

LeDoux, J.E. (1989) Cognitive-emotional interactions in the brain. *Cognition and Emotion*, 3(4), pp. 267–289. https://doi.org/10.1080/02699938908412709

Lomborg, B. (2012) Environmental alarmism, then and now: the Club of Rome's problem – and ours. *Foreign Affairs*. July 1. https://www.foreignaffairs.com/articles/2012-07-01/environmental-alarmism-then-and-now

McNeill, W.H. (1976) *Plagues and peoples*. New York, NY: Anchor Books.

McCall, S., Vilensky, J.A., Gilman, S. and Taubenberger, J.K. (2008) The relationship between encephalitis lethargica and influenza: a critical analysis. *Journal of Neurovirology*, 14(3), pp. 177–185. https://doi.org/10.1080/13550280801995445

Nelson, R.H. (2010) *The new holy wars: economic religion vs. environmental religion in contemporary America*. University Park, PA: Pennsylvania State University Press.

OECD. (2012) *Cybersecurity policy making at a turning point: analysing a new generation of national cybersecurity strategies for the Internet economy.* https://www.oecd.org/sti/ieconomy/cybersecurity%20policy%20making.pdf

Patterson, K.D. and Pyle, G.F. (1991) The geography and mortality of the 1918 influenza pandemic. *Bulletin of the History of Medicine, 65*(1), pp. 4–21.

Prechter, R. (2016) *The socionomic theory of finance.* Gainesville, GA: Socionomics Institute Press.

Prechter, R. (2004) Sociometrics—applying socionomic causality to social forecasting. *The Elliott Wave Theorist*, September, pp. 1–12.

Prechter, R. (1999) *The wave principle of human social behavior and the new science of socionomics.* Gainesville, GA: New Classics Library.

Prechter, R. (1994) Expectations for the Grand Supercycle bear market. *The Elliott Wave Theorist.* March (Special Report).

Read, K.A. (1986) The fleeting moment: cosmogony, eschatology, and ethics in Aztec religion and society. *The Journal of Religious Ethics, 14*(1), pp. 113–138. http://www.jstor.org/stable/40015027

Rogers, K. (2020) 1968 flu pandemic. *Encyclopedia Britannica.* March 25. https://www.britannica.com/event/1968-flu-pandemic

Spreeuwenberg, P., Kroneman, M. and Paget, J. (2018) Reassessing the global mortality burden of the 1918 influenza pandemic. *American Journal of Epidemiology, 187*(12), pp. 2561–2567. https://doi.org/10.1093/aje/kwy191

Thompson, C. (2023) Humanity at risk? Fear of technology rises with negatively trending social mood. *The Socionomist*, July, pp. 2–10.

Viboud, C., Simonsen, L., Fuentes, R., Flores, J., Miller, M.A. and Chowell, G. (2016) Global mortality impact of the 1957–1959 influenza pandemic. *The Journal of Infectious Diseases, 213*(5), pp. 738–745. https://doi.org/10.1093/infdis/jiv534

Weber, M. (1992) *The protestant ethic and the spirit of capitalism.* London: Routledge.

AFTERWORD

Prechter's theory and its legacy

I view Robert Prechter's thinking as a combination of realism and metaphysics. In his theory, he turns the linear, one-dimensional and mechanistic explanation, into a nonlinear and probabilistic interpretation of reality. In practice, this means the secondary nature of "why" type of questions. To understand the social world, you do not have to know all its working mechanisms. Indeed, Prechter rejects mechanism as a useful lens through which to understand society, opting instead for his socionomic model which combines worldviews of organicism and contextualism. Metaphysical waves of social mood are the *causa prima*, the first cause, for fluctuations in the tenor and character of aggregate social behavior. Where this enigmatic natural rhythm originates remains a mystery, though it appears in mimetic human interaction and becomes visible in herds. In its turn, realism in socionomics is the method of observing the world. If observed sociometers seem to indicate the existence of a certain mood, then the tenor and character of resulting social trends can be predicted probabilistically, even before they actually happen.

If it looks like a duck, swims like a duck, and quacks like a duck, then it probably is a duck. This method is called abductive reasoning and it applies to subject's habitual characteristics. In socionomics, interpretation of human expressions such as trends in fashion, music, movies, politics, scientific discoveries, etc., takes place by identifying the overarching social mood contexts, reflecting optimism or pessimism, in which they occur. This interpretation of references resembles the ability used by art experts in their work to understand phenomena in arts on a broad scale.

Since socionomic theory represents an entirely new paradigm, few researchers in the humanities or social sciences have yet heard or are aware of it. The theory is probably best known in the field of behavioral finance,

DOI: 10.4324/9781003387237-7

as applications of the theory to financial markets have appeared in behavioral finance journals and been presented at the field's scholarly conferences. Scholarly work that applied the theory to social behavior beyond the markets, such as presidential elections and Russia's military resurgence, has also been published in peer-reviewed journals. However, as a pioneering theory, socionomics has mostly been ignored by critics.[1] Perhaps this situation will change as new research becomes available on the subject. No doubt the theory's validity and ability to explain social trends will be questioned. Although socionomics may be considered an intriguing hypothesis, my experience is that many dismiss it almost automatically and without even understanding its premises or investigating it further.

The idea that the socionomics could serve as an all-encompassing model of how society really works may seem overly simplistic to many. The single most important reason for this skepticism about socionomics is still probably this: A deep understanding of the theory's clear and even simple principles requires an entirely new way of looking at the world, while socionomics challenges orthodox, linear assumptions about cause-and-effect in society. Social mood precedes action, but social action and external factors do not affect the social mood. Internalizing this principle idea is not an easy task, and it may take some time to fully comprehend, as it requires letting go of what is taken usually for granted.

In addition to this, the theory's elements that pertain to financial markets, what Prechter calls the socionomic theory of finance, are diametrically opposed to the Efficient Market Hypothesis (EMH). EMH is one of the dominant models of financial market pricing in academic finance, as discussed in Chapter 2. According to EMH, financial markets are efficient because prices already reflect all information about the stock or other securities and prices quickly adapt to new information. In contrast, the socionomic ideas that the prices of financial assets are regulated by social mood[2] and that information is used only by the conscious mind to rationalize pre-existing mood-induced imperatives is incomprehensible to proponents of the Efficient Market Hypothesis.

Since the process of herding is known in biology in animal populations, the idea that herding instinct would apply to humans seems likely. In other words, although socionomics might still be seen as a hypothesis, new scientific discoveries and advances of technology will tell us evidently in what extent the theory is correct. In the same way that meteorology is a science, socionomics studies emergent phenomena. As scholars and other fields have predicted volcanic eruptions and earthquakes, socionomists have predicted social unrest.

Although the human lifespan is usually relatively short, it is amazing how rarely people benefit from the experiences of past generations. As socionomics puts it, the social mood is endogenous and unremembered. However, from an individual perspective, an enlightened reader can personally observe the social mood and act on it as they see fit. Many of us have noticed significant technological, economic and cultural changes around us, and socionomics provides a context in which to understand them and anticipate what is likely to come next as waves of social mood unfold.

The idea of waves in human behavior is of course nothing new. One of the most famous historically cyclical theories, the theory of long waves was presented by the Soviet Russian Nikolai Kondratieff (1892–1938) in 1920s at the Moscow Institute of Economic Research. His official task was to prove the correctness of Marx's economic theory and investigate the mechanisms that would inevitably lead to the collapse of capitalism.

According to Kondratieff, the development in capitalist societies can be visualized in periods lasting on average 54 years. These episodes include four seasons: spring, summer, fall and winter. Unfortunately, the Kondratieff ended up with a statement that was wrong according to the communist party: even if the economy in capitalism goes through a crisis from time to time, he found that it is not destroyed, but every depression always contains the seed of a new rise. Stalin did not like Kondratieff's thoughts and thus he was captured and taken to Siberia, until he was finally executed in 1938 at the Kommunarka shooting range in Moscow. In Kondratieff cycles, each economic cycle has its own characteristics and innovations:

Kondratieff first cycle (1780–) was the hydropower, textile and the time of mechanical industry. The second cycle (1830–) was based on the mobility brought by steel and railways and the development of markets brought with it. In the third cycle (1880–), the electrical and chemical industries accelerated

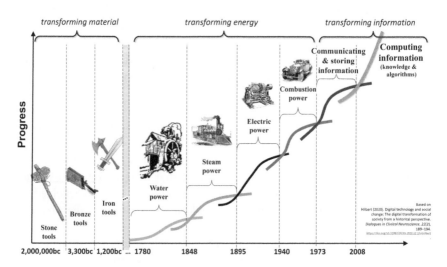

FIGURE 6.1 Kondratieff's cycles.

the development of cities, while the fourth cycle (1930–) was powered by the petrochemical industry, from cars to airplanes and finally to space rockets. The fifth Kondratieff wave began in the 1970s, when the development of telecommunications has been central. In the sixth wave, innovations are sought in new forms of energy, digitalized health care and environmental and nanotechnology.

Regarding the seasons of the post-World War II era, my interpretation is as follows. The optimism that developed after World War II in Western countries was reflected in the birth of the baby boomers between 1945 and 1950. The period that followed this, the 1950s and 1960s, can be compared to spring, while society and culture were also strongly renewed. After the short back winter, i.e., the recession of the 1970s, the 1980s and 1990s can be compared to summer. The prosperity and standard of living achieved at that time have not really been surpassed in Western countries (for the middle class) since then. The first signs of autumn can be dated to the events of 2001 and 2008 and, at the latest, to the slowing down zero interest rate economy of the 2010s. Is the end of the great era of prosperity in Western liberal democracies near? It seems that countries are trying to postpone the inevitable by taking on unprecedented debt. As a result, we are heading for a cold winter.

The forecast that a cold winter is coming for Western financial markets when the current era of expansion ends accords with Prechter's outlook, which is based not on Kondratieff wave analysis but on Elliott wave analysis. According to Prechter,

> The Elliott Wave Principle and the Kondratieff cycle are entirely different models. The Wave Principle is a behavioral pattern that is not tied to periodicity. The Kondratieff is an economic cycle of inflation and deflation that lasts approximately 54 years.[3]

However, Prechter understands that the two models can co-exist as useful descriptions of human behavior, writing that

> Although [the Kondratieff cycle] has averaged 54 years in duration, cyclic periodicities can expand and contract and are therefore inherently unreliable for precise timing. But the sequence of events within the Kondratieff cycle may be an immutable social process, regardless of how many decades it takes to play out.[4]

I note another key similarity between the two models: they each suggest that no matter how deep a financial crisis gets, eventually prosperity will return.

Chapter 2 of this volume addressed Prechter's use of the Elliott Wave Principle as a descriptive model of social mood fluctuation in his career as a social theorist. In these final paragraphs, I briefly consider Prechter's use of the

Elliott wave model as a tool for stock market forecasting in his career as a technical market analyst. Market forecasting is, of course, an entirely different discipline from social theory. Nevertheless, it is noteworthy that the same individual has applied the model in both domains.

Although the Elliott wave model has been used by technical financial market analysts for decades and the model is useful for forecasting the market, not everyone in the market forecasting industry necessarily believes in it. Historically scientific development is often and repeatedly underestimated. The utility and validity of the Wave Principle for market forecasting will be tested only in practice.[5] Meanwhile, research confirms that the Wave Principle is feasible and the waves can be recognized with a pattern recognition method based on neural networks.[6]

According to Prechter (2016), five practical realities affect the utility of the Elliott wave model for real-time financial market forecasting. These are "the probabilistic nature of potential wave paths, the degree of clarity in the waves, the analyst's degree of competence, biases of the analyst, and analysts' own impulses to herd in contexts of uncertainty".[7] He notes that dealing with these difficulties takes immense effort – and most people do not do it well, many people cannot do it at all, and no one does it well all the time.

Since stock market forecasting is based on probabilities, some schools of thought, such as EMH, even suggest that such forecasting is impossible regardless of the method used. Because the stock market is a complex dynamic system, it can exhibit emergent behaviors that are not shared by any of its components. Emergent behavior can occur on a macroscopic scale that people who look at only the microscopic scale of the individual would have no idea about it. And, of course, stock market forecasting is always carried out in an environment of uncertainty. In other words, financial market prediction is certainly difficult. However, that something is hard to do does not mean that it cannot be done.

Prechter's first book, *Elliott Wave Principle—Key to Market Behavior*, was published in 1978. Writing in the depths of the bear market of the 1970s, he and co-author A.J. Frost forecasted a wildly ebullient financial asset mania that would rival if not exceed the stock mania of the 1920s, followed by a spectacular financial bust that would rival if not exceed the Great Depression of the 1930s[8]. The first part of this forecast has come true to an extent greater than even Prechter imagined.[9] Yet, despite many "worst since the Great Depression" moments in the markets and economy in the ensuing decades, the fulfilment of the latter part of the forecast has remained elusive.

Nevertheless, Prechter has held firm in his long-term market outlook,[10] writing, "It has never been a matter of whether we would experience a tremendous bull market followed by a historic bear, only a matter of timing and extent".[11]

However, Prechter is not the only analyst to make these sorts of claims. Many cyclical thinkers, such as Ray Dalio, talk about cycles, cultures and monetary systems, and warn of the likelihood of significant trouble ahead. While massive fiscal borrowing is transferring ownership to the very richest, and investment and economic activity are slowing down, an increasing number of people get their living in the form of various subsidies. At the moment, inflation and interest rates are rising. Central banks do not dictate the movements of interest rates; socionomic research shows that they follow the movement of interest rates set on the open bond market.[12] Will we see the tide of inflation turn to deflation as the nominal values of assets melt, real estate and stock prices collapse, and geopolitical instability, authoritarianism, possibly wars and other global shifts in the balance of power occur? Good reasons why this would not happen are most welcome.

Although such a situation is rare, it is not entirely exceptional in history. Socionomic theory seems to provide plausible accounts of not only historical phenomena but also the phenomena we have witnessed in recent years: epidemics, authoritarian control measures, travel restrictions, trade and business restrictions and other disturbances. The internal political polarization, the large national debts all over the world and the geopolitical tensions are phenomena that all reflected a serious transition in social mood. The question is, what happens next? Will the social mood trend rebound to become more positive and usher in a further era of peace and prosperity? Or will mood become more negative and realize the worst of our fears?

Another question is if Robert Prechter's long-term prediction as a market analyst fails, should we abandon his separate work as a social theorist and thereby reject socionomics? I don't think there's any reason for that. However, if his socionomic view turns out to be correct, it will change our understanding of how society works and what its members are fundamentally like.

Notes

1 For a response to one of the scant works of criticism that the theory has attracted, see Chapter 41 of Prechter (2016).
2 Sornette and Johansen (1997, 420). In their study of large financial crashes of 1929 and 1987 the researchers come to conclusion that that crashes have their origin in the collective "crowd" behavior that have an endogenous origin whereas exogenous shocks serve only as triggering factors. Socionomics, on the other hand, proposes that all aggregative financial market price activity, including crashes, has an endogenous origin. Consistent with other research, socionomics rejects the notion of exogenous shock triggers of market trends.
3 Kendall (1996/2018, 47).
4 Prechter (2002, 113–114).
5 For example, see Atsalakis, Dimitrakakis and Zopounidis (2011).
6 Volna, Kotyrba and Jarusek (2013).
7 Prechter (2016, 146).
8 Frost, A.J. and Prechter, R. (1978/2017).

9 See the foreword to Prechter (2002).
10 For Prechter's latest market forecasting monograph, see Prechter (2022).
11 Prechter (2002, xxii).
12 See Prechter (2016, 73–80) for details and historical evidence of central banks' tendency to follow the bond market.

References

Atsalakis, G.S., Dimitrakakis, E.M. and Zopounidis, C.D. (2011) Elliott wave theory and neuro-fuzzy systems, in stock market prediction: the WASP system. *Expert Systems with Applications, 38*(8), pp. 9196–9206. https://doi.org/10.1016/j.eswa.2011.01.068

Frost, A.J. and Prechter, R. (1978/2017) *Elliott wave principle—key to market behavior.* Gainesville, GA: New Classics Library.

Kendall, P. (1996/2018) *Prechter's perspective.* Gainesville, GA: New Classics Library.

Prechter, R. (2022) *Forecast for the Bear, 2022–2024 and beyond.* Gainesville, GA: New Classics Library.

Prechter, R. (2016) *The socionomic theory of finance.* Gainesville, GA: Socionomics Institute Press.

Prechter, R. (2002) *Conquer the crash: you can survive and prosper in a deflationary depression.* Hoboken, NJ: John Wiley & Sons, Inc.

Sornette, D. and Johansen, A. (1997) Large financial crashes. *Physica A: Statistical Mechanics and Its Applications, 245*(3–4), pp. 411–422. https://doi.org/10.1016/S0378-4371(97)00318-X

Volna, E., Kotyrba, M. and Jarusek, R. (2013) Multi-classifier based on Elliott wave's recognition. *Computers & Mathematics with Applications, 66*(2), pp. 213–225.

INDEX

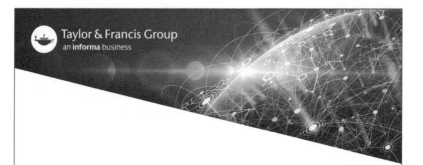